"Self-Publish Your Own Book"
- a (simple) Guide

Yale Class of 1963 Authors

" SELF-PUBLISH
YOUR OWN BOOK "

A (SIMPLE) GUIDE

Sterling Memorial Library

YALE -
CLASS OF 1963 AUTHORS

Yale UNIVERSITY LIBRARY

"Self-Publish Your Own Book"
- a (simple) Guide
Yale Class of 1963 Authors

Authored by: Jon Hadley Larson

Authored with: Yale Class of 1963 Authors

All rights reserved:

Copyright: © 2014 by Charity Enablers Foundation

  dba The Jon and Karen Larson Family Foundation

  a California 501(c)(3) corporation   www.lff1.org

  FEIN: 68-0460563   CA-02237360

6" x 9" (15.24 x 22.86 cm)

 262 pages

ISBN-13: 978-1497388925

ISBN-10: 1497388929

LCCN: 2014906294

BISAC: Language Arts and Disciplines > Publishing

"Books"...... by Barbara Wertheim Tuchman

*"Books are **the carriers of civilization**.*

Without books, history is silent, literature dumb, science crippled, thought and speculation at a standstill.

Without books, the development of civilization would have been impossible.

*Books are **Engines of change**,*
*   **Windows on the world**,   and*
*   **Lighthouses erected in the sea of time**."*

"This is a very worthwhile project. I think that you are addressing interests and curiosities that are shared by many people in addition to our classmates."

Bob Flanagan - *The Perilous Life of Symphony Orchestras*

"Above all, I am stunned by the quantity and quality of books that have come from our class and are collected in this compendium.
Keep writing!"

William Nordhaus - *The Climate Casino*: Risk, Uncertainty, and Economics for a Warming World

Dedication:

- I have been most fortunate and blessed to have shared my last 50 years with **Karen Brown (Larson),** as deep, complex, intelligent, funny, mysterious, strong and loving a woman as God ever placed on our green earth. I thank her for enriching my life beyond imagination by gently exposing her love of knowledge and her world of books to this old Yale engineer.

- My two sisters **Helen** and **Gail** have both enriched my life immeasurably.

- No father is prouder of his son than I of **Derek** and his wife **Hien**.

- Being a grandparent (for me to **Zach** and **Annie**) truly is God's reward for our often difficult life's work here on Earth. I am blessed with two voracious readers in any format they can get, books and eBooks alike, and both are fledgling writers as well.

Acknowledgment:

- The **Wikipedia Subject Matter Experts** who contribute resources to the extensive, growing and widely referenced Wikipedia database of knowledge used in this book.

- The skilled **Software Writers** and **System Integrators** for creating the ability for us to self-publish our own books.

- **Marjorie G. Dunstan**, a Punahou English teacher (1940-1975) who was my 9th grade English teacher in 1956, and all of the skilled teachers who dedicate their lives and careers to teaching us to read and write good English and to appreciate good writing.

- Our **Yale Class of 1963 Classmates** whose published books inspired me to want to contribute one of my own and who collaborated on this book to provide future self-publishers the benefit of their wisdom and experience.

Contents:

Part I   Parts II & III

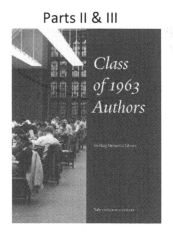

Books by Jon H. Larson

Published:

"Self-Publish Your Own Book"　　　　　ISBN: 1497388929
a (simple) Guide - with the Yale Class of 1963 Authors

In Progress:

"Talk Story"　　　　　ISBN: 1499343191
Growing Up in Hawaii in the '50's

"Stay Loose"　　　　　ISBN: 1499344090
An (almost) Complete History of Humor

"Live Long and Deep"　　　　　ISBN: 1499344104
Wisdom of the Ages

"Continuing Adult Education"　　　　　ISBN: 1499344127
Staying Fresh and Current Through Technology

"Wake Up Call" - America (2014 – 2036)　　　ISBN: 1499344134
Surviving and Prospering in the 4th Crisis Era in Our History

"Swimming with Sharks"　　　　　ISBN: 1499344165
Angel Investing in the Ocean of Venture Capital

"Family Foundations Are Fun"　　　　　ISBN: 1499344196
Forming and Running Your Own Family (non-profit) Foundation

"Roles in Life"　　　　　ISBN: 1499344233
The Roles Men and Women Play in Our Lives

Preface:

This book seeks to encourage, motivate and enable readers to Self-Publish their own book(s).

It is a thorough, comprehensive, understandable and up to date presentation of the resources and technologies of the Self-Publishing industry that are available today to the first time Self-Publisher.

Part I - "Self-Publish Your Own Book"

is an easy to follow step by step Guide that you can follow to self-publish your own book. It walks the reader through the process using the new generation of low cost and simple to use tools and services available online over the Internet to:

1) **Complete your book into publishable form**.
Physical form as a Hardcover or a Softcover book, and in Digital form as an eBook.

2) **Introduce it into the distribution channels** that will generate you sales, revenue, and recognition and celebrity.

3) **At minimal cost to yourself**.

Part II - Yale Class of 1963 Authors:

presents a collection of more than 100 books published by 81 Yale Class of 1963 authors, spanning an almost inconceivable variety of subject matters -- literary, artistic, musical, medical, legal, religious, scientific, historical, mathematical, political, autobiographical, and many more. It is a striking display of the many directions in which Yale 1963 classmates have taken their talents since graduation over a half century ago.

Part III - Collective Wisdom of the Published Authors:

Wisdom, Tips and Advice from experienced Yale Class of 1963 published authors are shared with the reader.

<u>Notes:</u>

Introduction:

As a young lad growing up in Honolulu, Hawaii, I was fortunate to attend Punahou School. Founded in 1841, Punahou is one of the oldest and the largest independent school in the United States today. It was founded by Protestant missionaries from New England including from the Yale School of Divinity (Yale itself was founded in 1701) with a Christian teaching mission. Punahou maintains a Christian focus from its founding missionaries. Its programs have been broadened over the years to embrace an enhanced interfaith spirituality emphasis and approach.

A religious program was part of the curriculum. We shared regular weekly chapel services, a required course in Religion 101, and a full-time pastor employed on campus who was accessible to all of the students. In 1953, then school Chaplain Kenneth Rewick took our class on an Interfaith tour designed to expose us to the facilities and leaders of other faith traditions including a Buddhist temple, a Shinto shrine and a Jewish synagogue near the campus. At the synagogue I recall the Rabbi discussing with me the importance of each of us leaving a legacy. He made it sound simple, and I have carried his words with me all of my life.

"To achieve your own legacy, you must do three things:
1) Father a **Child**, 2) Plant a **Tree**, and 3) Write a **Book**."

I would like to believe that I am a successful and loved grandfather which of course required me to take the interim step and help to bring my own child into the world and give him the roots and wings to be successful. I have planted countless trees over the years, at homes in California and in Nebraska where our Omaha neighbors nicknamed me "Sam Arbor" from the large number of trees I planted on our newly built tract home in a former cornfield. I am the co-founder and chairman of the _Iliahi Foundation of Hawaii_ we formed in 2000 with the vision and mission to plant and nurture rare and endangered native trees to maturity in the forests of Hawaii. But my legacy was a two legged stool because I had been unable until now to complete step 3), write a book.

Like each of us, over the years I have accumulated much wisdom I wish to pass along to future generations as part of my legacy.

Now into my early 70's, I am running out of years to perform. I created a web site *Larson Family Foundation* listing the non-profit organizations that I have nourished over the years and which have nourished me in the process. That required significant up front expenditures of cash, special programming skills, and an ongoing cost to maintain the site which will remain current only until I pass on.

I have eight mostly completed books stored in my desktop computer at home that I have written over the years, needing only final assembly with a word processor to ready them for publishing; *Growing Up in Hawaii in the 1950's, *An (almost) Complete History of Humor, *Ageless Wisdom, *Continuing Adult Education, *Wake Up Call - America (2014 – 2036), *Surviving and Prospering Through the 4th Crisis Era in Our History, *Swimming with Sharks: Angel Investing in the World of Venture Capital, *Forming and Running Your Own Non-profit Family Foundation,* and *Roles Men and Women Play in Our Lives.* To date I have not completed any of these books due to not knowing how to take that important final step to publish and distribute my books.

That task seemed insurmountable and kept me at bay these many years from completing one of my life's main objectives, publishing a book. Until now. At my 2013 Yale 50th reunion, I came away newly inspired by the published works of over 81 of my 1963 classmates including significant recent books by David Boren, William Nordhaus, and John Lahr, and aware of the plans of classmates to publish more books. I vowed to myself I would publish at least one book before my 55th Reunion in 2018. Now thanks to self-publishing, I am considering publishing all eight.

As with all journeys to the unknown, and with only a general idea of where I wanted to end up, (published), I took the first step. I used my internet search engine and keywords *"self-publish."* Up came a list of 93,400 entries in 0.14 seconds of compute time.

Suddenly my world had changed. New possibilities emerged. But how to capitalize on my findings from that massive group of resources out there? I did a quick search and picked one system that appeared to be well documented, full function, cost efficient and organized.

I took that first hardest step and logged onto the site. Within three days I was able to self-learn the system, document my learning in digital form as I went, and get my book submitted in publishable form, (not counting a week wait for the LCCN Library of Congress Control Number).

The total cost to me? $95.00.

($49.00 for the LCCN Library of Congress Control Number, $7.00 for the initial prototype softcopy for final review, plus $39.00 for the first ten softcopy books mailed to my home). This first book is the result.

I used the Yale 1963 book collection already in digital format I had inserted as a section in _www.yale63.org_, the web site I created and maintain for our class. I enhanced it with more public domain descriptive information off the internet for each book and added several more recent books by Yale classmates including my Alaska fly-fishing companion John Lahr's _Tennessee Williams: Mad Pilgrimage of the Flesh_, and _Profiting from the World's Economic Crisis_ written by my San Francisco/Bay Area sailing companion Bud Conrad. And I added the Appendix section on manuscript grammar, style and formatting.

I added the section from my notes accumulated over several days as I learned how to publish this book using one of the many low cost resources available to us today over the Internet. I wrote a short book description. I wrote a short Introduction and an author's background for the cover. I located three .jpg photos for the cover. And I walked slowly and steadily through the documented ten step process, one step at a time, to publish this book in five days over a 10 day period.

Based on my own experience, it is my belief that using this Guide, and assuming your book is written and formatted, you can successfully:

- **Self-publish your own book,**
- **In 2 days of work,** (plus 5-7 days wait for the LCCN),
- **At minimal cost to you.** (under $100.00*)

(*includes LCCN number, one proof softcover and ten softcover copies mailed to your home). This assumes you have medium computer keyboarding skills and do not retain any of the optional consulting services. Publishing in eBook format would cost an optional additional $79.00 and in hardcover form an optional additional $99.00 for conversion assistance, and take an additional 2-3 weeks waiting after submission for conversion completion and approvals.

This book has three parts plus an appendix:

Part I -   "Self-Publish Your Own Book"
Part II -   Yale Class of 1963 Authors
Part III -   Collective Wisdom of the Published Authors
Appendix: Guidelines for Manuscript preparation,
            and the Knowledge Based global economy

Part I - "Self-Publish Your Own Book"

is an easy to follow step by step Guide that presents a successful proven template model which can be followed by each of you to publish your own first book. It walks the reader through the process and clearly documents the new generation of low cost and simple to use tools available at minimal initial cost over the Internet to:

1. Create your first book in publishable form.
2. Introduce it into the distribution channels that will generate sales, revenue, and recognition and celebrity to yourself.

Part II - Yale Class of 1963 Authors

presents a collection of more than 100 books published by 81 Yale Class of 1963 authors, spanning an almost inconceivable variety of subject matters -- literary, artistic, musical, medical, legal, religious, scientific, historical, mathematical, political, autobiographical, and many more. It is a striking display of the many directions in which Yale 1963 classmates have taken our talents since graduation over a half century ago.

Many of these books were published some time ago prior to the availability of the Internet and desktop publishing personal computing and self-publishing capabilities. Most used the more traditional book publishing methods. Some of these books were self-produced using the new tools available today that can take a completed manuscript and quickly get it published and distributed as a hardcover, softcover or as an eBook over the Internet.

The Yale Authors provided comments on their own writings. Book description comments (from various internet sources including Amazon, Barnes & Noble, and Google Books) have been included along with the cover jackets where publicly available. Almost all of these books can be purchased online in hardcover, softcover or electronic eBook form.

This book collection was first compiled by Laton McCartney and Guy M. Struve for presentation at Yale's Sterling Memorial Library for our 50th Class Reunion in 2013. It was enhanced by myself and merged with a section documenting the self-publishing process designed to create this educational Guide to motivate, encourage, and enable classmates and others to self-publish their own books.

Part III - <u>Collective Wisdom of the Published Authors</u>

This section describes some of the experiences getting published and makes recommendations to the first time self-publisher;
- The trials and tribulations of dealing with agents, publishers, reviewers and critics,
- Hesitancy to self-promote,
- Lack of keyboarding skills,
- Relevancy of our material in today's world,
- Book publishing courses (classroom and online).

The **Appendix** includes helpful information including; 1) preparing and perfecting your manuscript for submission as the input document to the self-publishing process described herein, 2) Distribution Channels, 3) maximizing Royalty income, and 4) Knowledge Growth Trends.

Synergy: "The whole is worth more than the sum of its parts."
Synergy is an observed phenomenon of nature where the interaction of multiple elements in a system produces an effect greater than the sum of their individual effects. The term synergy comes from the Greek word synergia, συνεργός, meaning "working together."

The published books in this collection individually each serve for all time as a record of achievement and contribution to our society and well being from each author. The synergy is powerful when the individual works are presented together as a *synergistic* whole, a contribution to mankind, where the whole endeavor is worth more than the sum of the parts because it serves as a teaching and inspirational model to others of what a group can achieve working together.

Getting started:
You too can be successful and self-publish that First Book you have already formed in your mind, parts of which are probably already stored in your desk top computer and the rest in handwritten notes.

Each one of us has some unique knowledge that needs to be published for the good of us all. You are hereby invited, encouraged (and challenged) to add your first published book to the total compendium of knowledge documenting and enhancing the human race. And to make it available instantly worldwide.

Once you learn and master the steps in this Guide to successfully publish and distribute your first book, it will become not a task to be avoided but an almost effortless joy to self-publish more books by yourself into a personal collection, from you the author for all of us, that contains your valuable wisdom, insights and contributions.

If it is not written and published in a distributable form, it is lost with you at your passing. Written in digital form as a book and published and distributed and available worldwide, you achieve a legacy which you and yours and we will appreciate and enjoy forever.

We wish you success using this Guide to assist you to self-publish your own First Book. And hopefully other books to follow.

All the best,

Jon H. Larson
Tiburon, California

and the Yale Class of 1963

Part I: "Self-Publish Your Own Book"

Contents   Page

Part I - "Self-Publish Your Own Book"

Historical context - looking back:

In the good old (pre-internet) days, publishing a book was a really big deal. Even after the heavy duty work of planning, organizing, writing and editing your book, you then faced an even greater hurdle to get it published.

- It required months and often years of research, planning and hard work.
- It required getting your own agent because publishing companies would usually only deal with agents who themselves only rarely dealt with unknown new authors.
- Your book was only available in hard and softcover form requiring a large and expensive minimum initial print run due to high setup costs. There were no lower cost eBook options.
- Books had to be priced high to cover the publisher's costs in the event the book was not as successful as planned.
- It was expensive. Assuming you were able to retain an agent and get the approval of the Publisher to publish, typically a range of $8,000 to $40,000 had to be committed to the first print run by you and the publisher, without knowing what the demand for your book would be.

With the evolution of:
- the **Internet**
- Powerful desktop **Personal Computers**
- Pre-packaged easy to use **Writing and Publishing software**
- **Print on Demand** technology (in units of one and only when ordered)
- **Integrated full function service companies** (pay as you use)
- **Mobile computing** (high quality hand-held Personal Digital Assistant PDA electronic reading devices)

many new and lower cost alternatives are now available to those of us wishing to publish our first book. And the market and our royalty profits for our books are larger due to reduced cost per book and to sales and marketing services built into the distribution/delivery systems that are provided by full service self-publishing companies using the Internet today.

Pre-personal computing: Before the 1980's, you hand wrote your notes and transcribed them word by word on a typewriter or to a transcription service. Or you hired a ghost writer. Editing and changes involved retyping or re-transcribing parts of the document.

Type fonts were limited. Insertion of photo images involved special manual "cut and paste" labor involving expensive experts and equipment. And the Index and the Table of Contents had to be manually built.

The advent of **Word Processing** on desktop personal computers combined with the photo processing capabilities of digital imaging software made writing a book much easier, assuming one possessed or had access to good keyboard skills.

The advent of **Online Publishing** software in the past ten years that is powerful and easy to use has greatly reduced the cost and the time and effort needed to publish your completed book. These new publishing systems are available in **two forms**:

1) **Purchase** the book writing software and run it on your own personal computer, and then use a separate **Print on Demand** service to distribute your book.

2) Use one of the **Online services** which integrate production formatting, editing, review, submission, print on demand, the internet distribution capability using the Internet Cloud, and the revenue accounting, all in a single vendor system solution, priced on an as used basis, with very minimal initial up-front investment/cost.

The packaging of expensive software and making it available over the Internet via 2) above (called **SaaS** for **Software as a Service**), instead of requiring a dedicated standalone computer and software package, has opened the door to fast, low cost and convenient self-publishing. This new integrated SaaS based industry service is the main subject of this book. There is a **large and growing list of companies** on the internet who can assist you with publishing your book. To see a list, just Bing or Google *"publish your own book"* or enter *"eBook software"* on Ask.com, and see the large list of resources available to you. Another excellent site to see what is out there is the professional networking membership organization at *http://authoru.org/.*

I did a cursory search and evaluation of many of the fully integrated publishing software packages and the online services available. I decided to go with approach 2) above, a fully integrated "one-stop shop" service, available online over the Internet as SaaS, (Software as a Service), with no up-front cost to get started.

Today and looking forward:

Once your book is **written** and stored on your personal computer, you can be **published** and have your completed book available online for sale as a softcover trade book, **within several days**, for **minimum cost to you,** and with your own **unique ISBN number** and **Library of Congress Control Number**. Ordering a review copy will be $7.00 more, and having the publishing company issue your LCCN number instead of doing it yourself will cost another $49.00. The total is $56.00 so far. Getting an LCCN is optional but probably worth the added expense. Sound interesting? Read on.

Getting started:

We suggest that your first book be a test. Create a short book (it must be at least 24 pages). Walk through all of the steps. And only then start working on your first production book.

Just log on and go, experiment, try steps, everything can be undone or changed. Use system supplied images and formats where available. View the results and then iteratively make changes and resubmit your book for editing/review. Then print your first softcover book and have it delivered to your home for around $7.00, your total cost to that point. It will not be published until your document has passed the editing requirements and you respond that you are ready to go. Your test can be deleted after you are familiar with the system and are ready to publish your first real book.

Ancient wisdom says that *"Every journey begins with the first step."* Taking that first step forward is the hardest step of the entire journey. This will be the case in self-publishing. You need to take that first step towards publishing your own book. Using a good self-publishing online service and following the steps in this Guide, you will quickly make a mole hill out of the mountain you perceive to be the effort in getting published.

My first book was published in 1969. Titled a daunting "*IBM System/360 TOPS Systems Integration and Test Manual*," it was a technical set of instructions for running a large IBM System/360 mainframe test of software prior to putting it into production. It involved keypunching each line of text on a card using an IBM 029 keypunch and manually sorting thousands of lines (cards) into 1000 card boxes of cards. The cards were then run manually through an IBM 2780/1403 RJE card/printer workstation to print the book. Updating the manual involved pulling a card, re-punching and reinserting it into the box of cards at the right location. The 1403 printer was a technological marvel. Print slugs raced noisily around a moving track band and were struck at high speed by hammers, a far cry from today's quiet laser printing technology. Crude but effective for the time, my publishing technique won an IBM award for "*creative use of technology.*"

I had been thinking about publishing my own series of books for over 20 years. In 1991 my first book attempt failed due to I could not get an agent in spite of over 20 contacts because I had no previous track record of publishing. The book manuscript and the agent brief still sit on my shelf today, "*America 1991 - Wake Up Call,*" emphasizing the key role that technology would play in the rebuilding of our education systems of the future which included *DataSpirit/2000*, my design which in 1991 was a precursor for the Internet to come.

Neither could I get my 2nd book published, "*CAE – Continuing Adult Education,*" about the failure of adults to keep up as the total knowledge of the world was doubling every 15 years (back then), and how online education can partially fill that void.

Undaunted by these previous failures, I forced myself to sit down and log onto Createspace and start the process because I wanted to publish this book to guide and encourage more of our Yale 1963 classmates and others to publish in order to leave legacies for myself, our families and each other, and for future generations.

This was my first book published. It was published in five days work over ten days using the information presented in this Guide, with no advance study. I requested a LCCN number which took an additional week waiting for issue by the Library of Congress. Knowing what I learned and have presented in this Guide, I believe I could have done it handily in aggregate two days plus the wait time on the LCCN.

Assuming you have reasonable keyboarding skills or have family members or grandchildren who can type for you, and using this book as your guide, there is no reason why you can't accomplish the same. In this book we use (**hardcover** and **hardback**), and (**softcover**, **softback** and **paperback**) interchangeably. And we use **eBook** to refer to all digital electronic forms of a book distributed over the Internet and read on mobile handheld electronic devices I still call PDA's for Personal Digital Assistants. Some designate the word **paperback** as a cheaper form for fiction and a **softback** or **softcover** as a less expensive form for a more weighty subject hardcover book.

Two basic steps are required in the publishing process:
1) **Write** your book
2) Get it **Published**

This Guide assumes you have completed step 1) above, have already written your book, and it is stored as a manuscript on a computer file in completed digital format in *Word* or *Adobe* or *Pages,* ready to go.

Now on to the meat and potatoes of Self-Publishing your book.

There are **four major components** you must acquire or use via a service:

1- Writing software: (for composing your document in digital form).

2-Publishing software: (to integrate the cover and the document into completed digital form suitable for production printing).

3-Print on Demand: (hardcover and softcover books in units as small as one to match actual sales as they occur and to eliminate expensive warehousing).

4-Distribution and Accounting:
    a. U.S. Mail – (hardcover or softcover)
    b. Electronic Distribution over the Internet (eBooks)
    c. Getting paid for each book

1- Writing software: (for composing your document)

Microsoft **Word** and Adobe **Incopy** are two of the most used software packages for word processing. **Pages** for Mac is another. Over the years each has added numerous features so that they now allow you to produce a fully digital form of your manuscript to submit along with your supporting information and your book cover to your printing distribution company. This book was composed at home using Word 2007 on a Gateway *All-in-One PC* platform running Windows 7.

2- Publishing software:

Integrates the cover and the document into a completed digital form suitable for production printing. Four of the well established Self-Publishing products and companies presented herein are:

- Serif   PagePlus X7 Publisher
- Adobe   InDesign Creative Suite
- Scribus Open Source Desktop Publishing
- Quark   Xpress 10

3- Print on Demand:

from Wikipedia

Print on Demand (POD) is a printing technology and business process in which new copies of a book (or other document) are not printed until an order has been received, which means books can be printed one at a time. While build to order has been an established business model in many other industries, "print on demand" developed only after digital printing began because it was not economical to print single copies using traditional printing technology such as letterpress and offset printing.

Traditional publishing was revolutionized by the advent of print on demand services. As the digital age advanced and new printing and printer ink technology became available, the approach to publishing changed.

Print on demand has been successful because unlike traditional publishing, the technical setup is much quicker, and costs are reduced due to elimination of inventory storage costs. Print on demand has also become a popular means of creating customized business cards, greeting cards and a variety of other media.

4- Distribution

U.S. Mail – (hardcover or softcover)
Electronic Distribution over the Internet (eBooks)

www.Books.Google.com
Amazon.com/Books
www.BarnesandNoble.com
www.ibooks.com

are four of the many companies who have built large databases of millions of books for sale over the Internet. Many hundreds of thousands of these titles are available as eBooks for purchase and for immediate download to your desktop computer or your mobile device.

Using *CreateSpace.com* as we did to produce this book title, our book is stored online and available for sale worldwide through the Amazon.com Books library, Kindle Direct Publishing, and other distribution channels. The book description you provide and an image of your cover are displayed along with pricing information and independent comments/feedback evaluation ratings from book buyers. Your book is maintained in an index for searching by interested book buyers. Your book can be priced separately for the eBook download, softcover and hardcover. eBook pricing is the lower cost option, softcover the middle tier cost, and hardcover pricing will be the highest cost. The distribution vendors will help you to price your book based on b/w or color, page count and delivery format (electronic, hardcover or softcover).

Mobile computing:

At times it is very nice to curl up in a cozy corner or in front of the fireplace or stretch out on the beach in the warm sun, and page through a book. We are used to holding the print media in our hands and paging through at our own pace.

With the advent of Mobile computing and hand held display devices (I still call them PDA's or Personal Digital Assistants) as the IPad, Kindle, ChromeBook, Nook, and the MacBook-Air, we can now page through a handheld device at our own convenience.

But instead of purchasing the content from a bookstore online, we now can simply download it quickly over the internet or the cell phone network to our reading device, at prices generally significantly lower than for a physical book. It costs pennies to send electrons over fiber-optic and wireless networks ($0.30 for this book as an eBook) instead of expensive resources consumed for printing, binding, packaging, paper, ink, warehousing and transportation costs of traditional book production and distribution ($4.00 for this book as a softcover). Technology and the Internet have opened the doors to this new way of producing and distributing print media.

Vendors offering self-publish services:

An internet search using keywords *"self-publish your book"* turned up many tens of thousands of entries related to these keywords. There are many companies and people in this fast growing industry.

Below are eight of the excellent self-publishing print on demand services along with self-descriptions of their services.

1. AuthorHouse   *www.authorhouse.com*

"Book publishing is our passion. Through professional design, editing, and marketing tools and consultation, AuthorHouse has become the most respected alternative to the traditional publishing route. From top-notch design and editing services to online distribution, one-on-one author support to innovative promotional campaigns and platforms, you can rest assured that your book will receive the VIP treatment it deserves. Not only that, AuthorHouse helps you to forge your own literary path and take your book wherever you want to take it—to the bookstore, Hollywood, or various networks."

2. iUniverse   *www.iuniverse.com*

Packages www.iuniverse.com/Packages/StandardCompare.aspx

"With iUniverse, you can publish your book, your way—today! Our top-quality publishing, editorial and marketing services make it simple for writers just like you to quickly and affordably publish professional-looking books. Affordable publishing packages. Packages start at just $899! Professional publishing, editing and marketing services. We help you make your book the best it can be and find its audience. Global distribution. iUniverse books are available for order from online book retailers worldwide including Barnes & Noble.com and Amazon.com. Nonexclusive contracts. We don't own your copyright—you do! Experience and dedication. Our executive team has more than 65 years of combined experience in the publishing industry."

3. Xlibris   *www.xlibris.com*

"Xlibris is a book publishing company created by authors, for authors. By focusing on the needs of creative writers and artists and on how print-on-demand technology and new approaches can be applied in the publishing industry, we are able provide authors supported self-publishing services that will help them see their books in print. Whether you are writing a book, promoting your work, or searching for online publishing services or a self-publisher to publish your book, Xlibris's comprehensive range of publishing, editorial, add-on, and marketing services enable you to customize your self-publishing experience. Our team of publishing professionals are available every step of the way to guide you throughout the publishing process."

4. Blurb *www.blurb.com*

"We love beautiful books. Which is a good thing, because beautiful books are our business. And helping you make your book with our tools—no matter what that book is or your reasons for making it—is our passion. We can print just one book for you—or a thousand. Want to sell your book? You can do that with us too. And we make it easy to share and promote your book if that's your thing. Want to make a personal photo gift book? Invented here. Are you an author? Welcome. Want to make a book for your business? You're in the right place."

5. Lulu *www.lulu.com*

"Lulu is a generalist print on demand publisher who will print books; calendars; photography books; brochures and even comic books. The advantage of using Lulu is that there are no setup fees and they even offer additional services such as editing; marketing tools and advice, and press releases which are very handy for a first time author who has little or no experience in publishing and marketing."

6. Printondemand   *www.printondemand-worldwide.com*

"Welcome to Printondemand-worldwide, your complete publishing solution

Printondemand-worldwide has almost two decades worth of trading experience, proudly making us one of the UK's longest established digital book printers. Our customers range from high-street and academic publishers to authors self-publishing their first work. We are constantly investing in the latest printing technologies, as well as evaluating the market, and anticipating our customers' needs, in order that we attract and maintain our business relationships to the fullest. Whether you are a small, medium sized or large publisher, we can work with you, to understand your needs and we think you'll agree we have plenty to offer."

7. Spiderwize   *www.spiderwize.com U.K.*

"Our publishing package now also includes us sending you copies of the electronic design files (cover and interior) of your book for you to keep for your own records (at no extra cost). We will send you these once your book has completed production. We know of no other POD publishing service which includes this in their package. We take your finished manuscript, professionally format it so that it's ready to print, design a great looking cover, assign an ISBN to your book, send it to our printers, and add your book to a US and UK distribution list. Your book will then be available to amazon.com, amazon.co.uk Barnes & Noble, Book Depository (Amazon UK Marketplace) and many more online shops and wholesalers. Our publishing package now also includes us sending you copies of the electronic design files (cover and interior) of your book for you to keep for your own records (at no extra cost)."

8. Bookstand Publishing   *www.bookstandpublishing.com*

"Bookstand Publishing has been helping authors self-publish since 1996.
With our publishing services you can publish and market your book to a world-wide audience in eBook, paperback and hardcover formats.
To work with us you simply chose the Publishing Package that best suits your publishing needs, submit your manuscript and our expert team will format your book, design a cover, set up an e-commerce page, and print and fulfill books orders for you as they come in.

You retain ALL rights to your book. We accept Rough Format manuscripts.

Our Classic and Custom Book Publishing Packages include all of the following:

- Published within 8 weeks
- Author retains ALL rights

- e-Commerce Web Page for your book
- Softcover or Hardcover edition of your book
- Kindle, Nook and Epub (Apple IPad) editions of your book
- Bookstand Publishing handles all order fulfillment
- 30% royalty on cover price sold from your e-Commerce page
- 70% royalty on Kindle eBooks sold, 50% royalty on all other eBooks
- Full color cover from a single provided image
- ISBN registration number
- Bar code
- Electronic proof
- Printed proof
- Author wholesale discount rates
- Included in Amazon, Barnesandnoble.com and most online retail stores
- Choose from four publishing packages:

-Classic Publishing Package $499
-Custom Publishing Package $699
-Premium Publishing Package $2,499
-Executive Publishing Package $4,999

Other vendors who offer self-publishing services:

1) *Full Service Self Publish*
www.OutskirtsPress.com

2) *Print Your Book in 2 Days*
www.48HrBooks.com

3) *Self-Publish Your Book*
www.abbottpress.com

4) *Publish Your Own Book*
www.morrispublishing.com

5) *Self-Publish Your Book*
www.LifeRichPublishing.com

6) *Christian Self Publishing*
www.masterpressbooks.com

Evaluating which service to use:

From the many fine systems and companies out there, we selected www.CreateSpace.com. CreateSpace is owned by Amazon, having acquired and merged *BookSurge* and *On-Demand Publishing, LLC*. CreateSpace uses Amazon to distribute books prepared using its services and also links you to Kindle Direct Publishing for eBooks and to other outside distributors. CreateSpace appeared to meet our initial requirements which included the following:

1. Minimal cost to get started.

2. A complete full function fully integrated support system available.

3. System is intuitive and can be self-taught.

4. Human consulting support is available for a reasonable cost when needed upon request.

5. Fully integrated with the production and distribution services of Amazon.com for eBooks availability through Amazon's Kindle service.

6. Services for printing and sale/distribution of both soft cover or hard cover books.

7. They do the billing function, collect proceeds and distribute royalty profits automatically to the author's bank account directly or via snail mail check.

8. Minimal cost for getting published initially. There is zero cost until you decide to sell hardcover or softcover books other than two optional costs:

   -$7.00 to purchase a final review proof hardcopy,

   -$49.00 to have the provider get you an official LCCN Library of Congress Control Number (optional), or you can do this yourself at no cost. Beneficial if you plan to sell to Libraries.

Ten steps to getting Published:
(using an online service such as CreateSpace.com):

1. **Produce your book offline** using your word processor. Typically Microsoft Word or Adobe InCopy or Apple Pages. You can download a preformatted template from CreateSpace with pagination and titles and chapter headings pre-inserted to help you format your book components. Otherwise you can use your book file as you created it offline, doing the sections, chapters, and page numbering yourself.

2. **Familiarize yourself** with the process by reading available documentation similar to what has been provided here.

3. **Logon to www.createspace.com** and create your unique Member *userid* and *password* and supply basic information. If you wish, supply your bank account information for automatic deposits of book proceeds on a regular monthly basis as they are earned. They will also snail mail checks each month provided the total is over $100.00. This and most other data can be skipped over initially and added later.

4. **Create the account** for your first book using your book title as the project name.

5. **Design your internal document and cover** frontispiece, front and back with title and supporting descriptions designed to quickly gain the interest of a potential buyer/reader. You can use your own .jpg photo images or use standard images provided. It is suggested you have three image files ready to download: 1) a photo of yourself as the author, and 2) an image for the cover of your book, and 3) an image for the back of the cover. Select whether you want color or black and white. The file parameters for the book page size and layout must match the parameters you used when you created your document. Standard print page sizes are: 5.5 x 8.5, **6 x 9**, 7 x 9, 8 x 10, and 8.5 x 11. We suggest you start with 6" x 9" standard, and Calibri or Verdana font, size 11 or 12. Full left and right Justification is preferred for text alignment, with a 1.1" page inside margin and a 0.5" page outside margin.

6. **Submit your files** to CreateSpace.com with the cover design.

7. **Checking and review** is then done automatically by computer and manually by staff who will let you know where any formatting problems exist that need to be repaired for the best presentation.

8. Specify **initial printing/distribution methods**;

(a trade softcover, a hardback cover, or an eBook online, or any combination of the three). Initially you will want to order several softcover copies at a discount to the author to give to family and friends who will all be very impressed they now have a "published author" in the family. You also specify if you want your book to be distributed through the library, bookstore and book club routes.

And once you are published…..

9. **Marketing and promotion:**

10. **View the book sales statistics** reported to you on your CreateSpace "*Dashboard*" as sales are generated. **Watch your cash income build** in your bank account as sales proceed and you prepare to publish your second book.

Basic Book choices:

You need to make the initial choice about your book:
1. Type: **Softcover**, Hardcover, or eBook
2. Interior: **b/w** (black and white) or color
3. Paper color   **White** or Cream
4. Size   **6"x 9"**

Typically you will start with a softcover first, b/w interior type, on white paper. The cover will always be in color. You can insert color photos and images and text in your Interior document which will allow you to select color print options later even though you are starting with a b/w interior. There is a range of book sizes; we suggest you start with the most common, 6" x 9".

Cost considerations:

Each book type can be printed in either b/w or color. The softcover and hardcover printing costs run around $0.015 per page in b/w and up to $0.15 per page in color.

There is no cost differential to distribute an eBook over the Internet so your eBooks will usually be in color. There are optional conversion consulting service packages to produce follow on versions of your first softcover trade book; $79.00 for an eBook setup conversion from your softcover trade book. And $99.00 for a hardback version.

Since color printing costs run up to $0.15 per page, the b/w books are much less expensive to produce, $4.00 for this 262 page book in b/w, and est. $38.00 to print this book in color.

Five Steps before you start:
(using an online service as CreateSpace.com):

What you need to get started:
Prepare these materials first.

1. The full Title name of your book. Plus a second tag line to embellish the Title.

2. Your completed document in *Word.doc* or *Adobe.pdf* format. If *Pages*, save as a .pdf file. Title page, copyright page, Table of Contents, body, Index with pagination, chapter headers and numbering. Start to end, in completed form, exactly as you want it to appear in your book.

3. Three .jpg files.
   a. Photo of yourself, the author
   b. Photo to insert on the front page of your book cover
   c. Photo for a personal book logo (a 2nd photo image on the back of the cover.)

4. Book Description: 150-250 words

5. Author description: 150-250 words

Special notes before we get started:

1) The series of steps presented in this book is generic to almost every self-publishing product or service that you will use. This Guide presents the questions listed in the order expected by CreateSpace. Other self-publishing services will ask these questions in a different format and order, but most will require most or all of this information.

2) There are Help prompts, and additional information is available throughout all of the processes. This Guide does not recreate this information. It is intended as a high level big picture view from the top that walks you through the steps you will encounter. Whenever you have a question, you can usually click on a nearby Help prompt for a longer detailed description of the data element in question.

3) You can always return to your Dashboard which is the entry point for all of the areas to be addressed in building your book for self-publication. This is an iterative process, learning by doing, multiple times through. You can stop any time, save your work, and sign back on later and continue from where you left off.

Now let's get started:

Logon to   www.createspace.com

Create your own Member **userid** and **password.**

There are Seven sections to accomplish first:

     I. Create the project

     II. Interior

     III. Cover design

     IV. Distribution

V. Pricing

VI. Submit Files for Review

VII. Final Proofing and Release for publishing

And then looking ahead:

VIII. Future Versions
IX.   Marketing and promotion
X.   Going big time

I. Create the project:

You start at the **Member Dashboard.** This screen summarizes all of the links you will access to build your book. You will return here to start most of your sections and automatically each time you log on. It will show you the status of the progress of your book as you work each step towards completion.

Add a New Title:
Enter the project name which must be identical to your book name to be entered later

Softcover:
You publish your book in one of two forms; 1) Physical form as a Hardcover or a Softcover book, and 2) Digital form as an eBook. Your initial book form through CreateSpace must be Softcover. Later you can specify Hardcopy with dust cover, or eBook form as well.

Guided Setup:
Later when you know the system, you can speed up entry by clicking *Expert*.

Sub-title:
Added to your Title name as an additional description that also appears on your book cover

Name:
You the Author (or you can use a Pen Name if you want)

Add Contributor:
if you want to show names of any co-authors for credits

Edition #:
1 or leave blank. This can be used later for future follow on version editions your book.

Publication date:
Leave blank for now. The system will insert the actual date when approved by you for printing/distribution.

Save and Continue:
This saves your work so far. It can be easily updated later.

ISBN option:
The ISBN (**International Standard Book Number**) system is utilized to automate ordering and inventory systems for book publishers, distributors and retailers. It is also utilized for the monitoring of sales data in the publishing industry. Click on "Free-CreateSpace assigned." The 13-digit ISBN is assigned by standard book numbering agencies to control and facilitate activities within the publishing industry. Unless you have already applied separately and received an ISBN, just let the system assign one for you for free. Your machine scannable ISBN will be printed in bar code format on the back of your book cover for you.

II. Interior:

This section has to do with identifying the interior of your book, everything from the first to the last page; book title, table of contents, acknowledgments, preface, introduction, the full text, epilogue, appendix, bibliography, index, and the author's bio.

Type: b/w or Color
Paper: White or Cream

Page Size: 6" x 9" standard.   This is one of the most popular sizes these days. You can use any of the standard sizes offered. This book is 6" x 9". You must set the margins in your word processor for your interior book page to exactly match the specifications you select here for your book size. 1.1" inside and 0.5" outside left and right margins work fine to make sure that your text appears centered within the box template capability of the POD Print On Demand printer and that nothing appears outside the printable space on each page.

You have an option here to Download a standard book template which is a pre-defined outline form you can use to lay out your book. It has the sections, chapters and pagination pre setup and you can cut and paste your text into this template.

How to Submit:
Once your book is 100% completed offline and in a full text file format in Word or Adobe, click on *UpLoad – Browse* and select your book filename on your desktop. We suggest you use the .pdf format.

Notice that Professional Services are available (for additional cost) to help you here. Checking that box will get you a real person on the phone to assist you with this portion of your book entry. Then **Save:** your work so far. You should do this every chance you get to make sure that you do not lose any of your updates as you move along.

Launch Interior Review:

Issues list:
The first computer review of your interior submission will respond with an Issues List.

You will see such comments as:
"The book name does not match your project name.", or
"The book page size does not match the page size of your document."

You need to check and resolve each issue. You will see a red flag inserted in the specific area of the document where the error comment applies, making it easier to apply the proper resolution. You have the option to ignore errors and continue on with your cover design and return later to resolve any remaining issues.

III. Cover design:

Finish: Select *Matte* or *Glossy* finish   We like Glossy.

Cover Design:
    1) Build your own now   or   2) Use a cover prepared elsewhere.

You will most likely want to use cover design process 1). It provides a range of features and colors and templates from which to choose to create a very professional cover for your book at no cost.

Launch Cover Creator:
You will notice your cover (front and back) is presented on the upper right of the screen. An outline box will light up when you are working on any particular portion of the cover using the command prompts. Each change is updated as you go so you can see immediately how and where it will appear on the cover.

Select your template. This book used template #3;   *"Birch 6 x 9"*

13 steps for Cover creation:

Title: Identical to your Project name used earlier

Sub-title: Further describe your book subject

Author: Your name. You may use a pen name if you do not want to be bothered by the public acclaim from your successful first book.

Front Cover Image:
1) Select a provided image   or 2) Upload your own.
If using your own image, 5.25" x 7.5" at 300 dpi works best. Less than 300 dpi will not produce a crisp sharp image and the system will issue you a warning.

Fleurons:
Skip this step, (leave the Visible box checked). Fleurons are stylized forms of flowers or leaves used in publishing. There is a large base of public domain fleurons you can use in your book. Search on *"fleuron images"* on the Internet for public domain fleurons that you might

wish to use in your book. Fleurons can also be purchased from publishers and from individuals advertising on the Internet.

A Novel: Uncheck the Visible box unless you want *"A Novel"* to print on the back of your cover between the book description and the Author's background.

Book Cover Text:
   This should be between 150-250 words and be a bold and positive sales pitch that will quickly grab the interest of a potential buyer of your book. This very important statement will also appear in the book description section of the online book seller that potential buyers scanning your book on the internet will use to decide to buy your book or at least to research that possibility in more detail. Assistance in writing your book description is provided later in this section.

About the Author:
   This should be between 150-250 words and be a high level, interesting and "unhumble" description of what an intelligent, wonderful and unique person you are and why someone should be interested in reading a book written by yourself. Assistance in writing your Author description is provided later in this section.

Author Photo:
   1.5" X 1.5"   .jpg image   300 dpi

Author Bio: 150-250 words. Again, crisp, short, readable bullets.

Publisher Logo: Attach an image that describes who/what you are.

Background Color:
   Click within the color box on the upper left and select the color of your cover.

Submit Cover:
The computer will check your cover work so far and provide you with a template of how your cover will look with all of the information that you just keyed into the system. You can go back and change any of the input parameters to fine tune the appearance and content and images of your cover.

IV. Distribution

We suggest you proceed to section VI-*Submit Files for Review* now, and come back later to complete the Distribution/Pricing section described below.

Select the options for how and where you want your book distributed:
       o- In the U.S   o-In Europe   o-Through the vendor direct
             o- (any combination of all three)

Additional distribution services can be contracted, occasionally at additional cost, which will determine the lowest cost breakeven price of your book.
       o- Book Stores and Online Retailers

       o- Libraries and Actual Institutions

       o- Create your own Distributorship

After you are in initial production and sales have commenced from your softcover trade book and you have created an eBook or a hardcover version of your book, you have numerous options to expand the distribution channels for your book. These are discussed in the Appendix.

Save and Continue: (it is always a good idea to save your work often)

V. Pricing:

You can now calculate the price you want to charge for your book. Three variables must be balanced to set the best price level:
1) Your Royalty profit objective and expectation.
2) The cost the vendor will charge to print and distribute.
3) The market demand. Sales will be larger at a lower price.

The system will estimate the cost of the vendor to deliver your book to the Buyer. You can set the price you want to charge and the system will compute your Royalty for you, in U.S. $, Euro's, and the British

Pound. For example, the initial price I set for this book is $18.00 U.S. for the trade book version (6" x 9", softcover, b/w black and white interior, 262 pages). At that list price level, I make a royalty profit of about $7.00 per book sold, the vendor (CreateSpace/Amazon) makes a profit of about $7.00, while the cost to manufacture is about $4.00.

The eBook electronic distribution version of this book through the Amazon Kindle Store will be priced at $9.99 and my est. 70% royalty at that price level is close to $6.70 per eBook sold. The hardback b/w version would sell for $26.50 and I would make $6.70 at that price.

Amazon and other distribution channels will often discount your book from your list price. The initial publisher wants 20%, Amazon wants 20%, and other distributors will want up to 40%. Depending on which channel the Buyer uses to buy your book, the Royalty you receive will vary from as high as 70% down to 20% of your list price.

VI. Submit Files for Review:

If you are like all the rest of us, there will be some corrections to be made. The most common error is not to have completed one or more of the previous steps. You will notice on the left, the status of each required entry is indicated by a colored bullet circle; green is good, yellow indicates a potential problem that might need fixing, and no circle means you have not completed this required entry.

Just click on the entry that needs your attention. When all circles are green, click on Submit Cover again. It might take one or more iterations until you and the computer are happy with what you have supplied to build your cover.

All of your input is sent to the Cloud in the sky where it will be carefully reviewed, edited and checked by the vendor's software and human eyeballs for readability, printability and quality. This will take up to 24 hours, after which you will receive an email when the initial review is done.

The first results will be returned to you along with recommendations for improvement for quality and readability. If you are picture perfect your first time through, you are in an exceptional 1% of the population getting started with self-publishing. If you have one or more problems to correct, then you are among the 99% of the general population who, like myself, are learning challenged.

VII. Final Proofing:

In the proofing process you are looking for **formatting, design** and **grammar** issues. You have three methods to proof your book before you submit it for printing and distribution.

1) Use the **Digital Proofer** to see the entire book in exact published form.
2) **Print** the Interior and review it offline.
3) Order **a single physical softcopy final proof** to review offline at home. The cost typically will be under $10.00.

Use the **Digital Proofer** to preview the entire book in published form. This includes the cover and the full interior, and the complete book exactly as it will be printed in its final form.

It is suggested you do a complete review at least three times, each time focusing on one of the three considerations (formatting, design and grammar) to perfect your book and remove pesky errors that detract from the readability and professional quality of your book.

In the **Formatting review #1** you are looking at headers, footers, page numbers, spacing, table of contents, and the index.

In the **Design review #2** you are looking at images, captions, graphics, color, and the cover page.

In the **Grammar review #3** you are looking for punctuation and spelling errors. It is best here to download and review the interior document offline. When proofing our own writing, we often miss errors due to the way our brains are pre-wired. So be patient and thorough.

It took me 26 reviews to find every format, design and grammar error in my draft to submit for publishing. I fear there is still one hiding within that I missed. Rereading multiple times gets boring. You should enlist other(s) to proof read for you. You might be surprised at the grammar errors you missed. You are very likely to miss your own small typos because with multiple reviews, you get bored and lazy, speed up the rereading, continuing to miss very obvious errors that will cause a dagger to your heart upon first reading in your production book. Remember, **in self-publishing, you are the final editor**. The publisher will print anything you write, exactly as you write it, errors and all. Nothing detracts from the professional quality of a book like encountering a grammar typo. You want to be 100% accurate. So take the time and perfect your book. They say that in life, *"One gotcha undoes 1000 attaboys."* The same is true for typos in publishing.

It will be an iterative process where you will go back multiple times and make changes and repair errors. You will have the option to:

1- Make Changes and then   2 - Approve the Proof

As the final step in the proofing process, it is strongly suggested that you order one copy of your book to be delivered to you at home in its final print form. This will cost around $4.00 plus $3.00 shipping depending on the number of pages, and will be the best final proofing step to see the true look and feel of your book and to avoid the heart-stopping discovery of a glaring typo in your first production run.

Actually it is not as severe as it sounds. Even if you miss a typo you do not find until your first production print run, with CreateSpace you can easily make the correction and resubmit the manuscript. CreateSpace will immediately suspend sales for 24 hours until your new update is officially released, and sales will continue. There is zero cost for multiple resubmissions until you eventually get it right.

And remember those famous words…. *"To err is human…."* We almost never get anything right the first time. Zero defects is the desired end point, but not very realistic for a first go at anything.

It's Showtime: Time to publish!

When you are finally ready to go, you will now Approve the process to Distribute your book. This will be done according to the pricing and delivery alternatives you have chosen. The vendor will take over now and make its final arrangements to get you into production.

Your final step might be to purchase 5-10 copies of your book online, sign each one with a personal handwritten note from you, and ship them to family and friends. And send a copy to any key detractors (critics) who never thought you could do it. And of course place one in an obvious place in your book shelf by the front door or in your office where others will notice. The publisher will offer unlimited copies of the first print run at cost to you the Author. Ten copies of this 262 page book cost me $45.00 including shipping. The look on the face of one of my biggest critics and detractors upon receipt of his book….. Priceless!

VIII. Future Versions:

Based on feedback from the actual experience, you can repeat the process and install updates and additional material into your book and quickly produce the next version, at no additional cost to you. Over time you can iteratively produce multiple new and improved versions of your book and add chapters and content as you go, (and yes, repair any typos that missed your careful editing so you can sleep again).

IX. Marketing:

Once you have published your first book and it is available for others to purchase online (through Amazon.com if you used Createspace, or other online sellers/distributors), you are most likely experiencing a rush of excitement. You believe the hard part and the work are done and you are ready for the money from your book sales to start rolling in. But wait, there are no applause, huzzahs or accolades forthcoming. Instead, you find the silence is deafening. You probably purchased the first book yourself for validation, and maybe a proud family member or a friend or two also purchased your book, but otherwise no activity. Each morning you log on to check sales from the previous day. Surprise, Nada! Nothing! Zero! Zilch! Goose Egg! So you decide to wait a week. But still each morning is the same. No sales. Nothing. What went wrong? It is time for some serious reconsideration. There are some major problems in your way yet to be overcome;

1) Your book is showing up only on the site of the publisher. It can take 6-8 weeks to make its way through to other distribution channels.

2) You are not the first one to ever write a book. Authors are out there who have been publishing for years, many of them with five or more books to their credit. There are over 1.5 million books already out there in the marketplace, and thousands of new books are arriving in the market each month by authors as yourself. And maybe there are some well established best sellers in your own book subject category.

3) No one is finding your book. If they do come across it while doing a generic search on your book category, it will be buried far down

towards the end of the list of books in any search because the sellers list books by past activity indicating potential new sales. So until your book starts to get hits (looks) not even necessarily leading to buys, it will languish towards the bottom of any search list, be it Barnes and Noble, Amazon, or other. No one will find your book, even though it just could be the next best seller headed for the New York Times top 100 list.

This current situation (non-sales) can actually be quite depressing, especially coming off the high of producing your book and getting it published. Unfortunately, you have come to the realization that your work is not done. And in some ways, the real work, marketing your book, is still ahead of you.

Here are three must do's to promote your first book to help get sales started.

1. Get Good (*** 5 star) Reviews:**
Good reviews sell books. The more good reviews, the more books you will sell. The emphasis is on the word "good" here because any bad reviews of 3 stars or less will hurt sales. The better the reviews, the more books you will sell. So it is important that your first reviews be good ones. How to get good reviews? You need to sand bag the system in your favor. Others do it and you should also. Ask selected family members and good friends to make the effort to log onto the book distributor site and give it a good review.

There are ways to get copies to them to read. Email them your manuscript which could be a hefty 3-7 mb which today's email systems handle quite easily. Or purchase 25 books at the publisher's cost (typically $3-$4.00 each to the author) and hand them out to people who you believe will not only want to read your book but then will take the time to log onto the site and give you a 4-5 star review

Make sure you provide the one-click URL internet link access to the book review section of your distributor so they do not have to go searching for it. Send them some samples in your email of what you are looking for. In no case should anyone give you a review without first reading your book although this is possible. You don't need hundreds of five star reviews. Ten good reviews in the 4-5 star category is all you need to get launched.

2. Public appearances:
Public speaking is a great way to sell books. People like to buy books from people they know. When you speak, people feel as though they come to know you and thus become more likely to buy your book. You can take a card table and a stack of your $3.00-4.00 books purchased from the publisher direct, personally sign and hand them out at key opportunities. Look for opportunities to join book signing get-togethers at schools and other functions. Drop off copies to all of the libraries in your local area (assuming that you have made the extra expense of applying for the LCCN).

3. Build Key Relationships:
Today, more books are purchased online than through traditional bookstores. The key to making online sales happen is to establish key relationships with important websites, blogs, and e-zines. It is essential to build a bigger marketing platform so you can get your message out.

Summary: Initial marketing of your book sounds like a lot of work, and it is. It is going to cost you time, resources, and out of pocket expenses. But it is well worth the effort.

Self-Publishing-Check-List by Andy Baldwin is an excellent book you should consider to assist you in the essential areas of book marketing and promotion.

Put together a marketing plan in your project budget ahead of time, and realize that self-promotion is going to be required in order to establish a reputation and a solid track record upon which you can build a reputation that will help to get your book sales jump started initially until they can accelerate on their own through association.

Marketing your book can be great fun. Beyond your family and close friends who will be hugely impressed at your endeavor just getting published, you will network into a whole new and wider circle of associates, the exciting group of Authors out there. Authors as a group generally are very intelligent, deep observers of life, and extremely interesting people with which to deal. Publishing a book is an extreme art, and any published author you will find to have interesting things to day and will be interested in things that you have to say yourself.

Book readers are very interesting people as well, and you will be surprised how smart and friendly and inquisitive folks will be at book clubs and book signing functions. Once your book sales have commenced and have acquired self-momentum, you will quickly regain your confidence both in yourself and in what you have to contribute as your book sales tick up and royalty revenues start accumulating in your bank account.

X. Going big time:

If you are hugely successful, you can go on local and national book tours around the country, attend conferences, take professional publishing courses, be a featured speaker and a published "rock star," maybe even appear on TV, and continually enhance your expertise through contact with the self-publishing industry that is growing by leaps and bounds.

The big publishing houses watch the sales statistics for the eBooks and self-published trade books, and for better selling books will often make an offer to purchase the publishing rights outright, providing you the author with new aggressive avenues for promoting your book and an early out on the profits, providing funds to you for a well deserved vacation after which you can start your next successful book.

More Background on book types:

from Wikipedia...
A paperback (also known as a softback or soft cover) is a type of book characterized by a thick paper or paperboard cover held together with glue. In contrast, hardcover or hardback books are bound with cardboard covered with cloth. Although more expensive, hardcovers are more durable. Inexpensive books bound in paper have existed since at least the 19th century in such forms as pamphlets, yellowbacks and dime novels. Most modern paperbacks are either "mass-market paperbacks" or "trade paperbacks".

"Mass market paperbacks" (or MMPB's) are small, (relatively) inexpensive paperbacks sold through venues other than traditional bookstores: drug stores, convenience stores, airport gift shops, and so forth. The biggest giveaway is the bar coding: in a traditional book, the bar code on the back is the EAN "Bookland" code. It will typically have the ISBN written above it and will begin "978" or "979". In a mass market paperback, the bar code on the back will be a UPC code, and the Bookland EAN will be inside the front wraps.

Paperback editions of books are issued when a publisher decides to release a book in a low-cost format. Cheap paper, glued bindings, and the lack of a hard cover contribute to the inherent lower cost of paperbacks. Paperbacks can be the preferred medium when a book is not expected to be a major seller, or in other situations where the publisher wishes to release a book without putting forth a large investment. Examples include many novels and newer editions or reprintings of older books.

Since hardcovers tend to have a larger profit margin, publishers must balance the profit to be made by selling fewer hardcovers against the potential profit to be made by selling many paperbacks with a smaller profit per unit. First editions of many modern books, especially genre fiction, are issued in paperback. Best-selling books, on the other hand, may maintain sales in hardcover for an extended period in order to reap the greater profits that the hardcovers provide.

from CreateSpace:
With CreateSpace, you will initially be creating a trade paperback book, a softbound book that is usually larger and more expensive than a mass market paperback and is sold primarily online through Amazon.com books and in bookstores as a trade book. We do offer a Hardcover Upgrade service. With this service, we create a hardcover from your paperback printing files within 1-2 weeks; however, we currently do not offer hardcover distribution.

The Hardcover Upgrade includes a one-time setup fee of $99.00 per title and you can select 60# white or cream interior paper. You select one of the following binding options:

1- Case-bound laminate – hardcover book where the cover image is printed, laminated and bound directly on the boards that make up the cover of the book.

2- Library Cloth with Full Color Dust Jacket – hardcover book with a durable, navy cloth cover and a detachable, printed outer cover

Once the Hardcover Upgrade conversion is complete, you will be able to order hardcover copies at a wholesale rate which includes fixed and per-page charges. The fixed charge for each copy is $6.50 and an additional $2.00 for the library cloth with dust jacket option. Adding in the est. $38.00 color print cost, the cost to me per hardcover color book is closer to $50.00. And I would have to set myself up as a publisher on Amazon/Advantage and sell the hardcover version myself.

The per-page printing charge is $0.015 for a black and white interior. If the book has any color images or text within it, the book is considered full-color and the per-page printing charge is $0.15. A 150 page hardcover book in color could cost 150 x $0.15 = $22.50 plus $8.50, totaling $31.00, whereas a softcover with color printing will run around $21.50 and the same book in b/w will run around $3.00 to produce (print and bind). Given the cost economics of lower cost eBooks and softcover trade books, it is hard to justify dealing in hardcover books and is not recommended at this juncture getting started other than printing several as vanity copies for yourself.

So just start plain and simple, softcover, b/w print, and in the future you can add other hardcover and even color vanity versions paid out of profits from your softcover b/w book.

Kindle Direct Publishing (KDP): eBooks

KDP is a self-publishing platform where you can quickly and easily publish your book on the Amazon.com Kindle Store for a $79.00 one-time setup conversion cost. For more information, visit kdp.amazon.com/self-publishing/help. CreateSpace offers a Kindle Conversion service which converts your book files to Kindle-compatible files. To learn more about this service visit:
<u>Kindle Direct Publishing</u>

More Self-publishing background information:

from Wikipedia...

Self-publishing is the publication of any book or other media by the author of the work, without the involvement of an established third-party publisher. A self-published physical book is said to be privately printed. The author is responsible and in control of the entire process including, in the case of a book, the design of the cover and interior, formats, price, distribution, marketing and public relations. The authors can do it all themselves or outsource all or part of the process to companies (or individuals) that offer these services.

Self-publishing is not limited to physical books. Websites, eBooks, pamphlets, sales brochures, and other materials are commonly self-published. Audio books are growing in popularity and perhaps your first book can be rendered into an Audio book for special needs people by a company offering such services.

Business aspects of self-publishing:

The key distinguishing characteristic of self-publishing is that the author has decided to publish his or her work independent of a publishing house. In the past, self-published authors had to spend considerable amounts of money preparing a book for publication, and purchase bulk copies of their title and find a place to store them. Print-On-Demand and eBook technology mean the author, via numerous, accessible global distribution channels like Amazon.com, can have a book printed or digitally delivered – virtually world-wide – only when an order has been placed.

An October, 2013 analysis of U.S. ISBN data by ProQuest affiliate Bowker www.bowker.com revealed the following:

1) The number of self-published titles in 2012 jumped to more than 391,000, up 59 percent over 2011 and 422 percent over 2007.

2) Ebooks continue to gain on print, comprising 40 percent of the ISBNs that were self-published in 2012, up from just 11 percent in 2007.

3) The growing prominence of a handful of companies that offer publishing services to individual authors. More than 80 percent of self-published titles came to market with support from just eight companies, including Smashwords and CreateSpace.

4) "The most successful self-publishers don't view themselves as writers only, but as business owners. They invest in their businesses, hiring experts to fill skill gaps and that's building a thriving new service infrastructure in publishing."

Technological advances have enabled this growth:

- Print-On-Demand (POD) technology can produce a quality product equal to those produced by traditional publishers. In the past, you could easily identify a self-published title because of its poor quality. This is no longer the case.
- Online retailing where dominant players like Amazon.com have enticed readers away from bookstores into an online environment.
- Technological advances with eBook readers and tablet computers that enhance readability and allow readers to 'carry' numerous books in a concise, portable product.

Types of self-publishing:

Print on Demand   *POD*
Print-On-Demand (POD) publishing refers to the ability to print high-quality books as needed. For self-published books, this is often a more economical option than conducting a print run of hundreds or thousands of books. Many companies, such as CreateSpace, Lulu and iUniverse allow printing single books at per-book costs not much higher than those paid by publishing companies for large print runs. Most POD companies also offer distribution through Amazon.com and other online and brick-and-mortar retailers.

Electronic (eBook) Publishing   *eBook*

Preparing your manuscript for Ebook publication

In addition to the softcover b/w tradebook you produce as your first book, you should be planning from the beginning to produce and distribute an eBook version of your book because on average;

1) It could double your total book sales count, and
2) eBook royalties are very generous

Most manuscripts whose appearance is perfected only for book published print form do not transfer easily to the eBook format. A 400 page murder mystery or romance novel to be read from start to end, with no pictures, no formatting, a single font size, simple chapter titling and no need for indexing back and forth, will quite easily transfer to an eBook format and its appearance will be good.

However, more complex books containing a detailed referenceable table of contents, tables, photos, images, variable fonts, internal references to other sections of the book, and references to outside URL internet links, will not translate straight over and will need a considerable amount of reformatting to make the eBook as professional appearing and as readable as your printed book.

Most of us who are preparing to self-publish have a good to excellent experience level with working with word processors as MS Word, Adobe InCopy or Apple Pages to produce traditional WYSIWYG documents. But if you are planning to adapt your manuscript for publishing also as an eBook, you will need to acquire some new skills.

See the Appendix for more details on producing eBooks. For now, a good investment of your money and time getting started is _From Word to Kindle_: _Self Publishing Your Kindle Book with Microsoft Word, or Tips on Designing and Formatting Your Text So Your Ebook Doesn't Look Horrible (Like Everyone Else's) [Kindle Edition is $0.99]_ by Aaron Sheppard. This quick read will help you to understand why and how the tricks for formatting for eBook presentation can be built into your manuscript being prepared for printing and will greatly ease the production of a follow up eBook version of your softcopy book.

There are a variety of eBook formats and tools that can be used to create eBooks directly. The most popular formats are .epub, .mobi, PDF, HTML and Amazon's .azw format. Amazon.com, Barnes & Noble, Kobo and Smashwords all offer online tools for creating and converting files from other formats to formats that can be sold on their websites. Because it is possible to create eBooks with minimal up-front or per-book costs, eBook publishing only is an extremely popular option for self-publishers. Some recent bestsellers such as Hugh Howey's _Wool_, began as digital-only books. ebook.online-convert offers tools for converting your .doc and .pdf files to .mobi and other eBook formats required for input to self-publishing sites producing eBooks for distribution.

Vanity publishing   _Vanity Press_

The term 'vanity publishing' originated at a time when the only way for an author to get a book published was to sign a contract with a publishing company. Reputable publishing companies generally paid authors a percentage of sales, so it was in the company's interest to sign only authors whose books would sell well.

It was extremely difficult for the typical unknown author to get a publishing contract under these circumstances, and many 'vanity publishers' sprang up to give these authors an alternative: essentially, they would publish any book in exchange for a large payment up front from the author which assured a profit to the publisher. The term 'vanity publishing' arose from the common perception that the authors who paid for such services were motivated by an exaggerated sense of their own talent.

The line between 'vanity publishing' and 'traditional publishing' has, however, become increasingly blurred in the past few years. Currently there are companies that offer digital or print publication with no up-front cost. However, most of these companies also offer add-on services such as editing, marketing and cover design.

Self-publishing companies that fit this model include Lulu, iUniverse and CreateSpace. An author who simply hands his or her book over to one of these companies, expecting the company to make it a bestseller, would meet the previously established definition of 'vanity publishing,' but it's unclear how many authors fit this description.

Self-published best-sellers:

- Laurence Sterne's *Tristram Shandy* (1759–67) .

- Franklin Hiram King's book *Farmers of Forty Centuries, or Permanent Agriculture in China, Korea, and Japan* was self-published in 1911, and subsequently published commercially by Jonathan Cape in 1957, later by Dover Publications and has gone on to become an agricultural classic text.
- *Between the Acts* is the final novel by Virginia Woolf which was self-published by her Hogarth Press.
- Ezra Pound's *A Lume Spento* was sold by him for 6 pence each
- John Ruskin at the age of 11 sold a book of poetry he self-published with his father
- Other authors who self-published include Marcel Proust, Martin Luther, Walt Whitman, Emily Dickinson, Nathaniel Hawthorne, Jane Austen, and Derek Walcott.
- J. K. Rowling sold the eBook versions of the Harry Potter series directly from her website, Pottermore.
- In 2013 James Altucher's *Choose Yourself* sold 44,294 copies in its first month, is a Wall Street Journal bestseller and debuted at #1 on Amazon's top non-fiction list:

Title	Author	Notes
What Color is Your Parachute?	Bolles, Richard Nelson	Later published by Ten Speed Press
Chicken Soup for the Soul	Canfield, Jack	With Hansen, Mark Victor, co-author
The Christmas Box	Evans, Richard	
In Search of Excellence	Peters, Tom	
The Celestine Prophecy	Redfield, James	
The Joy of Cooking	Rombauer, Irma	
Poems in Prose	Wilde, Oscar	
The Wonderful Wizard of Oz	Baum, L. Frank	Later published By Reilly & Lee
Fifty Shades of Grey	E. L. James	Later published By Vintage Books

Self-Publishing software companies:

Self-Publishing is the art of publishing books and other printed material on your own whether through a professional printing service, usually an on Demand printer or at home. Additionally, publishing eBooks and other web publishing is also becoming quite popular as well. Either process requires the use of different software programs to guarantee a successful outcome including word processing software, graphics software, page layout software and electronic layout software, otherwise known as web layout software, although many programs now have the ability to complete all four parts of the process in one program called *desktop publishing software*.

What are the best desktop publishing software programs for self-publishing? The four professional desktop publishing programs below combine all parts of the process into a single program. All four are perfect for sending off digital copies of an author's finished work to an on demand printing press or for web publishing as well, allowing for the best results possible. These are four of the many excellent self-publishing print on demand services along with self-descriptions of their services followed by our own observations.

1) Serif PagePlus X7 Publisher - www.serif.com
"Desktop Publishing: Designing professional-quality documents, from cards to marketing materials, is fun and easy using our award-winning range of desktop publishing software. PagePlus, also enables you to fully edit PDFs, publish eBooks for iPad® and Kindle™, and make interactive multimedia brochures! Purchased online for $75.00. PagePlus is the most powerful and efficient desktop publisher yet. Accelerated Graphics Technology and support for 64-bit operating systems means PagePlus is faster than ever, especially important when designing large or complex documents.

PagePlus is here to help your business, charity or personal venture stand out from the crowd. Create posters, flyers, business cards, save and edit PDF files, and much more. PagePlus is the most versatile and easy-to-use desktop publisher ever! You don't need to be an experienced designer to put together professional and eye-catching promotional materials. Versatile templates and pre-designed assets such as graphics, frames and backgrounds, help you create virtually any type of document you wish. An integrated word processor, logo designer and photo editing lab make it easy to create attractive documents, while intelligent alignment tools give you neat layouts effortlessly, with no technical experience required. Whatever your organization, stand out and shine with PagePlus X7."

Page Plus X7 Publisher can be used to publish in print and web format, using interactive tools. Including thousands of templates in addition to graphic and text handling tools, some of the most useful features make editing easy. Logo and Image Cutout Studios create graphics and logos in addition to applying special effects to text projects and support for EPS and HD photos, duplex printing, drawing tools, native file sharing and more make this the all around perfect publishing tool.

2) Adobe's InDesign Creative Suite   www.adobe.com
"From books and brochures to digital magazines and iPad apps, InDesign CC (Creative Cloud) helps you create pixel-perfect page designs and typography. Easily adapt layouts for multiple page sizes, screen sizes, or orientations. It's part of Creative Cloud, so you can sync settings like keyboard shortcuts, presets, and workspaces across multiple computers."

Adobe is well known for great software programs with many features and functionality. Adobe's InDesign is a professional gold standard and it uses all of the main functions of its other programs, such as Photoshop, Illustrator, Flash and Fireworks, among others, into one simple to use publishing tool. InDesign is available for Windows and Mac operating systems as part of the Creative Suite (CS5) bundles or as a stand-alone program. This is one of the more expensive products but worth the price, especially if self-publishing of any kind is something a user does on a daily basis. Adobe is converting to a paid subscription model. Their publishing software is now available starting at $19.95 a month (at a minimum 12 month contract) ranging up to $49.90 a month for the full publishing package, allowing you to get started with a powerful system at a lower initial startup cost.

Adobe InDesign uses templates for web and print layouts, or the user can create his own, all of which integrates with other Adobe programs seamlessly. Main self-publishing tools include varying page styles and sizes, table creation, smart guides, text effects, drawing tools, 3D artwork controls, transformation tools and others. In using the InDesign user interface, it very much looks just the same as other Adobe programs do. Most of the controls are the same as well as is the functionality. If a user knows Photoshop or Illustrator, two of the most downloaded Adobe programs, they can use InDesign. This program is simple to learn and use with the help of online tutorials and Adobe's CS Live online services, both of which can help reduce the time in between the creation and publishing of works."

3) Scribus - www.scribus.net

"Scribus is an Open Source program that brings professional page layout to Linux, BSD UNIX, Solaris, OpenIndiana, GNU/Hurd, Mac OS X, OS/2 Warp 4, eComStation, and Windows desktops with a combination of press-ready output and new approaches to page design.

Underneath a modern and user-friendly interface, Scribus supports professional publishing features, such as color separations, CMYK and spot colors, ICC color management, and versatile PDF creation."

Scribus is an open source product and it has all the features of any pricey professional self-publisher, but is free of charge. While the design of the software and the user interface could use some improvements, it still does the intended job just as well as many other commercial programs. Scribus is available for all operating systems and offers online resources and documentation including user manuals, interactive tutorials and more. Some of the impressive productivity features and tools include graphic and logo editing tools, text effects, table creation tools, creating PDFs is a native function and a must have for all self-publishers. Technical support is available. This is a perfect replacement for many commercial self-publishing tools for jobs of all types and sizes."

4)   Quark XPress 10 Publishing Platform - www.quark.com

"We used to just create print but now we are ready to deliver content to print and Web, produce eBooks and even create apps for the iPad and other mobile devices. This is a publishing platform built for the 21st century and it's transforming how, when and where we communicate with our customers.

Today's customers demand engaging, relevant communications when and where they want and on their device of choice. Quark Publishing Platform is an end-to-end solution for enterprise organizations that enables meeting these demands while also reducing time to market and lowering costs. From a more efficient and compliant review and approval cycle to communication through the latest tablets and smartphones, Quark Publishing Platform automates your publishing. Content creators can use structured authoring while the rich design capabilities will empower your designers to create interactive, compelling communications. Customizable and able to integrate with existing business systems, Quark Publishing Platform will help you not only meet but also exceed your organization's goals."

Quark Xpress is a top end priced program, but it is worth the money considering all it can do. Xpress is a desktop web publishing software program, however it uses features of both Quark CopyDesk and Quark Print Collection and a shared content feature to produce finished works ready for on-demand print and web publishing.

Note: The features and prices quoted in the above packages and throughout this book are all subject to change. By this reading they could be significantly different than shown herein and must be checked with the vendors themselves for current pricing, features and availability.

SaaS - Software as a Service

SaaS is a software delivery model in which software and associated data are centrally hosted on the cloud by independent software vendors (ISVs) or application service providers (ASPs). It is sometimes referred to as "on-demand software."

SaaS is typically accessed by users using a thin client PC or MAC via a web browser. Besides book self-publishing, **SaaS** has become a common delivery model for many business applications including office and messaging software, DBMS DataBase Management software, CAD software, dDevelopment software, gamification, virtualization, accounting, collaboration, customer relationship management (CRM), management information systems (MIS), enterprise resource planning (ERP), invoicing, human resource management (HRM), content management (CM) and service desk management.

SaaS has been incorporated into the strategy of all leading enterprise software companies. SaaS is the way of the future for companies offering self-publishing services. Our vendor CreateSpace supplies help desk assistance personnel, computer cycles and data storage, computer operations, data backup, software design and programming. The vendor deserves to make a nice royalty on its considerable initial and ongoing investment and costs by charging a fair % royalty based on customer use of these expensive resources.

Getting help:

There are a number of people who want to assist you to be successful. Each of the companies offering self-publishing tools and services also provides assistance from the user community. Here are tips in three key areas to be successful:

    I. How to write an effective book description
    II. Guidelines for Writing Your Author Bio
    III. Adding Distribution Channels

I. How to write an effective book description:

by Richard Ridley *http://rwridley.wordpress.com/* on CreateSpace.
A writer for more than 20 years, Richard offers a unique perspective on book marketing based on his own experiences as a self-published author. "One of the most crucial elements to selling a book is also probably the most difficult element to create for authors. The book description is your lead in, your chance to hook a reader and get them to crack the cover and satisfy their curiosity. Even in an online environment, the book description can bridge the gap between having just another title among a sea of choices and a sellable book worth reading.   The problem is that many authors have a hard time writing a good book description. The main reason it can prove so difficult is because they don't want to leave anything out. As the creator of the material, there's a natural instinct to find a way to cram all or as much of that material into the description. But too many details can render your description confusing and ineffective.

Elements of the Book Description:
As someone who has failed and triumphed over book descriptions, here is what I have learned through my personal series of trial and error. Call them rules, suggestions or ramblings of an author gone mad, but I've collected these tips by observing and consulting with other authors, both self-published and traditionally published.

1. Don't include subplots.   When it comes to the book description, the only thing that matters is the main plot or main theme. That's all you need to focus on when you sit down to write your book description. Including anything else will send you off into an endless loop of "then this happened" moments that will dilute your book description. What is the primary action that drives your book?

2. Keep it under 150 words. This, no doubt, will elicit some moans and groans by a lot of authors. Summarizing a book that consists of tens of thousands of words to just 150 is impossible, right? No. In fact, I am of the belief that you should be able to summarize your book in a single short sentence. Remember, you don't have to concern yourself with the character development and sub-plots, so those tens of thousands of words it takes to adequately draw a reader into a book aren't necessary when it comes to your book description. In the simplest terms, what is your book about and what will make readers interested?

3. Write in third person, present tense. Even though your book is most likely told in past tense, your book description is not. You are describing this book as if you're sitting face to face with the reader, and they've asked you what the book is about. You wouldn't speak to them in the past tense. In addition, the book description is told from third person point-of-view even if you've written your book from first person point-of-view.

4. Use emotional power words. You are trying to evoke emotions with your book description, the same emotions that your book evokes. To convey these feelings, you need emotional powers words like tormented, charismatic, passion, obsession, and terrifying. There are too many to mention here, but a quick search for "Power Words" on the internet will produces hundreds of words to choose from. Just be careful not to overdo it. Use power words sparingly and strategically. If I had to put a number on it, I'd say in a 125 word description, you'd use 6-10 emotional power words.

5. You are not the author. You are not writing your book description as the author. You are writing it as the publisher. Making an impact on the reader is your principal concern. What will move the reader to want to know more about your book? What will motivate the reader to add your book to his or her cart? Write the book description with your head, not your heart. Remember, the book description is marketing material - not literature.

Another good practice when writing your book description is to read as many book descriptions in your genre as possible. It's a great way to figure out what the industry standard is. These descriptions become industry standards for one reason: they sell books. You are not just writing your description for your back cover. You're also writing this for your social media network, as part of your bio information for personal appearances, for flyers and other print material. This isn't just for you; it's for your fans.

With a concise book description, they are more likely to copy and paste it into an email to friends and family or on their own social networking accounts. Think of this type of description as being portable. It's easy to share and, as a result, is a major tool in your spread-the-word campaign."

II. Basic Guidelines for Writing an Author Bio:

"To many, writing an author bio is an enigma wrapped in a riddle buried with Blackbeard's treasure. It's hard to know what is and isn't relevant. What sets one author bio apart from another? Does work experience count? Is it accolades that matter most? What about education - does that make a difference? How can you express who you really are while meeting readers' expectations of you as an author?

The task of writing an author bio can be daunting because it is more than just information about the author. It is a crucial element in your branding strategy. *How* you present the information is as important as *what* you are presenting. Your bio is something many readers will see before ever reading your book, so its tone and verbiage may lead them to make assumptions about your book's contents.

The task of writing a bio isn't daunting if you know where to start and how to finish. Let's get started with some basic guidelines.

Distance Yourself. Embrace your multiple personalities, because your *author persona* is not writing your author bio. Your *marketing persona* is. You have to completely separate yourself from the author within and approach your bio from the third person. If a reader sees the pronoun "I" in a bio, he or she is likely to deduce that it's self-indulgent and amateurish.

You Are Your Genre. Before you write your bio, you must commit to a genre. It's important to understand what kind of book you have written in order to reflect readers' expectations. If you've written a dark horror novel, a bright, perky description of the author isn't going to help you reach your target fan base.

Always Be Branding. The author bio is essentially your business card. What do you usually find on a business card? Contact information. If you haven't given readers some way to get in touch with you, you missed the opportunity to interact with a fan, and interaction means everything in today's hyper-connected world. Give them a web address. Tell them where to find you on FaceBook and Twitter. You could even create an email address specifically for fan email. Give them access to you, even if it's just virtual access.

Keep It Brief. Brevity is the soul of wit. Even if you're William Shakespeare, you don't want to write an author bio that fills up the entire back cover. In an odd twist of logic, the more accomplished you are as an author, the shorter your author bio can be. Pick up a Stephen King or Cormac McCarthy novel and you're likely to see an author bio that's about 25 words. Pick up a book by an author you've never heard of, and you might see a bio that's 125 words. The more established the brand, the shorter the bio.

Be Humble. Establish a sense of humility to connect with the reader. In your bio, you are laying out a case to readers about why they should choose your book over another author's. Chances are, you have competition out there, so you have to walk the fine line of setting yourself apart without being a braggart.

Get Personal. Including some personal information in your bio is a good thing. If you have two kids and a dog that are very important to who you are as a human, include that information. Personal facts are a nice complement to all those incredible achievements you've included; it gives you depth and helps you make an emotional connection with the reader. If your list of achievements is somewhat lacking, the personal information that makes you who you are can more than make up for it.

Fiction vs. Nonfiction. There are key differences to writing an author bio for a fiction book and a nonfiction book. Nonfiction relies heavily on an author's credentials as it pertains to the book's subject matter, even if that subject matter is a memoir. How the author is an authority on the material is extremely important. Credentials for fiction writers can be important in the mystery and suspense genres. For example, an ex-police officer who pens a mystery novel can make a great impression on readers. However, one's education and experience outside of the world of writing is far less important in the fiction category. Bio's for fiction authors might do well to focus on the personal aspects highlighted above. Those basics will get you started thinking about how you will write your author bio. Remember, your author bio is a part of your brand, so make sure it is a reflection of who you really are as an author."

III. Adding Distribution Channels:

The contract for production of your book with CreateSpace.com and other self-publishing companies is typically a **non-exclusive contract** where **the Author retains all rights**. CreateSpace will automate sales and distribution of your completed book through Amazon.com Books and Kindle eBooks, once your book is produced, and will also forward your book to *Baker and Taylor*, and *Ingram* who will promote your book to numerous outside distribution channels. You can also use any number of additional companies and channels to distribute your book. You are free to select additional distribution companies as *Barnes & Noble*, *Apple iBooks*, and *Google Books* in addition to *Amazon*. Just make sure you are not signing over your ownership rights. See the Appendix for a more complete description of distribution channels.

Leadership Strategies in Book Publishing:

There are three other sources for self-publishers to get started:
   1. **Formal classroom courses**
   2. **Online courses over the Internet**
   3. **OWN Network**

1. Formal Classroom courses:
Two of the best courses you can take are offered at Yale and at Columbia.

Yale Publishing Course: Seminar on Publications

http://publishing-course.yale.edu

The publishing industry is changing at an unprecedented rate and it is increasingly difficult to keep up with emerging advances in technology and new business models. It is, therefore, more crucial than ever for managers to step away from their daily routines and reflect on the challenges facing them in a technology-driven world.

The Yale Publishing Course (YPC) provides this opportunity and you will emerge energized, inspired, and equipped with new skills to lead your organization more effectively.
Special features of the Yale Publishing Course:

- It is a course, not a conference.
- It is specifically geared to middle and senior level professionals.
- It is international in scope.
- It offers a unique curriculum.
- Its outstanding speakers, carefully selected for their expertise, teaching skills, and demonstrated performance as innovators, include leading publishing executives and industry experts as well as distinguished faculty from the Yale School of Management.
- It offers small group discussions and one-on-one access to speakers.
- Limited to 70 participants per program, it has a collegial and informal atmosphere.
- It takes place in a beautiful, state-of-the-art facility on the Yale campus.

Columbia Publishing Course: School of Journalism

http://www.journalism.columbia.edu/publishing

This is a six week course. For more than 60 years, the course has been training young men and women for careers as editors, literary agents, publishers, designers, publicists and more. Graduates can be found in every kind of job, at major magazines and publishing houses across the nation. If you are considering a career in book, magazine, or digital media publishing, the Columbia Publishing Course will give you the tools and the training you need to succeed:

- Broad exposure to current issues in publishing
- Unparalleled access to top publishing professionals
- Hands-on publishing experience
- Comparison of publishing types that informs career decisions
- Extensive career placement support
- Access to a large, active alumni network

2. Online courses and Blogs over the Internet:

Course online: (YouTube)
Best Amazon Kindle Online Self Publishing Course -
www.youtube.com/watch?v=vr7b8By5xgw

Blog postings:
Online Self-Publishing Course: Yay Or Nay?
http://catherineryanhoward.com

3. OWN Oprah Winfrey publishing network:

Oprah Winfrey has been a large promoter of reading and of self-publishing programs to her extensive audience. Her network offers this excellent source document for self-publishing information:
 http://www.oprah.com/omagazine/Publish-Your-Own-Book

On Selling Your Book:
"If you want to sell your books, pick a POD company that has an online store and will list you on Amazon.com's and Barnes & Noble's websites; and invest in a book or course on Internet marketing. A few industrious writers have sold as many as 5,000 copies this way—but they are the exception. To become a best-selling or prizewinning author, you'll need to find an agent and a traditional publisher."

Sterling Memorial Library - New Haven, CT

Acknowledgements
Yale Class of 1963

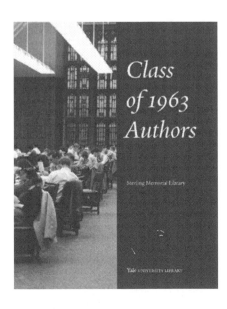

Part II - Yale Class of 1963 Authors

This collection contains more than 100 books published by 81 Class of 1963 authors, spanning an almost inconceivable variety of subject matters -- literary, artistic, musical, medical, legal, religious, scientific, historical, mathematical, political, autobiographical, and many more.

It is a striking display of the many directions in which our classmates have taken their talents since our graduation a half century ago. Authors have provided comments on their own writings. In addition book description comments from various internet sources including Amazon, Barnes and Noble, and Google have been included along with the cover jackets where publicly available.

Almost all of these books can be purchased online in hardcover, paperback, or electronic download form. We have included links here from Amazon.com but these books are also available for purchase on Google Books, Barnes & Noble, and elsewhere. This collection was first assembled by Laton McCartney with the urging of Yale to 50th Reunion chairman Guy Struve, for presentation at a Yale Sterling Memorial Library exhibit for the 50th Reunion of the class in 2013, a regular event sponsored at all Yale 50th reunions.

This compendium of books was further compiled and edited by myself into this Book designed to encourage 1963 classmates and others to publish our own books using the new electronic self-publishing tools available today.

These tools are relatively easy to learn and use. Their low cost allows for e-Publishing online and for printing, sales and distribution of both hardcover and paperback books, and for automation of collection and distribution of book proceeds to authors.

Proceeds will accrue through The Jon and Karen Larson Family Foundation, *www.lff1.org*, a private family 501(c)(3) foundation operated for public benefit charitable purposes only. Proceeds from the sale of this book will accrue to the Yale Class of 1963, Wikipedia, and LFF for promotion of Self-Publishing projects and for other best uses determined by the Yale 1963 Class Council.

Part II – Contents

	Page	Author	Title
26	103	Richard N. Foster	- Innovation: The Attacker's Advantage
27	104	Richard Friedlander	- Paradise Besieged
28	105	Michael Gates Gill	- How Starbucks Saved My Life: A Son of Privilege Learns to Live Like Everyone Else
29	106	Art Gilliam, Jr.	- One America: Moving Beyond the Issue of Race
30	107	Gerard Gold	- Business and Higher Education: Toward New Alliances
31	108	Donald Avery Graham	- Complete Works of Pir-O-Murshid Hazrat Inayat Khan
32	109	Thomas S. Greenspon	- Moving Past Perfect: How Perfectionism May Be Holding Back Your Kids (and You!)
33	110	DuPont Guerry	- Melanoma: Prevention, Detection, and Treatment
34	111	Larry Gwin	- Baptism: A Vietnam Memoir
35	112	Ridgway M. Hall, Jr.	- Hazardous Waste Handbook & All About Environmental Auditing
36	113	Michael Haltzel	- The Global Ramifications of the French Revolution
37	114	John Harper	- Cohomology
38	115	Stanfield Hill	- Plan Smart, Retire Rich
39	116	Alexander Paul Hixon	- Coming Home: The Experience of Enlightenment in Sacred Traditions
40	117	Robert Jacunski	- Quandary
41	118	Hewitt Jeter	- A Modeling Study of Gaseous Rn-222, Xe-133, and He-4 for Uranium Exploration
42	119	Philip A. Johnson	- Introduction to Business Data Communications with Broadband and Wireless
43	120	William F. Kay	- California Public Sector Labor Relations
44	121	Lindsey Kiang	- Huynh Phuong Dong: Visions of War and Peace
45	122	J. Robert Kirkwood	- Essentials of Neuroimaging
46	123	Michael Koenig	- Knowledge Management
47	124	Rob Lacy	- Diagnosis: Cataract
48	125	John Lahr	- Notes on a Cowardly Lion & Tennessee Williams: Mad Pilgrimage of the Flesh
49	126	Jon Larson	- Self-Publishing Your Own Book - a (simple) Guide Yale Class of 1963 Authors
50	127	Frank S. Letcher	- Mihail Chemiakin: Metaphysical Head: Deformation and Metamorphosis

	Page	Author	Title
51	128	Michael Lieberman	- Bonfire of the Verities
52	129	Thomas Lovejoy	- Climate Change and Biodiversity
53	130	Barry Lydgate	- French in Action: A Beginning Course in Language and Culture
54	131	Stephen MacKinnon	- Agnes Smedley: The Life and Times of an American Radical
55	132	Laton McCartney	- The Teapot Dome Scandal & Friends in High Places
56	133	Thomas H.McGlashan	- A Developmental Model of Borderline Personality Disorder
57	134	Williamson Murray	- A War To Be Won & The Making of Strategy & Military Effectiveness
58	135	William Nordhaus	- The Climate Casino: Risk, Uncertainty, and Economics for a Warming World
59	136	Robie MH Palmer	- Breaking The Real Axis of Evil: How to Oust the World's Last Dictators by 2025
60	137	Gordon Clark Ramsey	- Agatha Christie: Mistress of Mystery
61	138	Anthony Rhinelander	- Prince Michael Vorontsov: Viceroy to the Tsar
62	139	William Pennell Rock	- Performing Inside Out
63	140	John S. Rohsenow	- Modern Chinese Characters & Dictionary of Chinese Proverbs
64	141	David Rudenstine	- The Day the Presses Stopped
65	142	John R. Sack	- The Franciscan Conspiracy
66	143	Brian Salzberg	– Optical Methods in Cell Physiology
67	144	Stanton Samenow	- Inside the Criminal Mind
68	145	William F. Sanford	- The American Business Community and the European Recovery Program, 1947-1952
69	146	Murray Sargent III	- Laser Physics
70	147	Frederic T. Schneider	- The Art of Japanese Cloisonné Enamel: History, Techniques and Masters
71	148	Jerry Selness	– Primitive Benchmark: A Short Treatise on a General Theory of Sailing
72	149	Edward R. Shapiro	- Lost in Familiar Places
73	150	Harvey B. Simon	- Staying Well
74	151	Tom Stempel	- FrameWork: A History of Screenwriting in the American Film
75	152	Phillips Stevens, Jr.	- The Stone Images of Esie, Nigeria

	Page	Author	Title
76	153	Samuel N. Stokes	- Saving America's Countryside: A Guide to Rural Conservation
77	154	William D. Sudderth	- Discrete Gambling and Stochastic Games
78	155	Fritz Thiel	- Der Raum, wo nur als Geist du liebst
79	156	Gordon Thorne	- Area Collection
80	157	A.O. Dennis Willows	– Neurobiology and Behavior
81	158	Richard Worley	- Hypertension in Pregnancy

Yale Class of 1963 - "Books by Class Authors"

19 63

Sterling Memorial Library - New Haven, CT

Yale Beinecke Rare Book and Manuscript Library

Book Covers

19 63

Art Gilliam

Douglas Allen

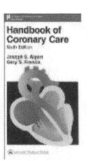

Joseph Alpert

Joseph Alpert

Walter G. Alton, Jr

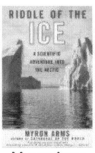

Myron Arms

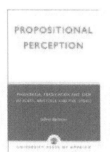

Jeffrey Barnouwe

Michael Davitt Bell   F. Michler Bishop   Stephen Bradley

  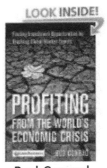

L. Paul Bremer III   Clifford Clark   Bud Conrad

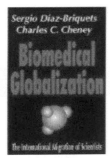 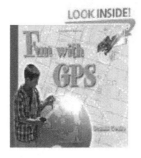 

Charles Cheney   Donald Cooke   David Bruce Cornay

Richard Bates Couser   Leo Damrosch   Edward Dennis

Robert Dickie   Anthony Elson   Norman Etherington

Carter V. Findley   Robert J. Flanagan   Richard N. Foster

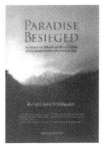  

Richard Friedlander   Michael Gates Gill   Thomas Greenspon

 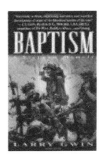 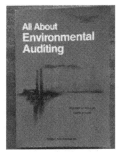

DuPont Guerry   Larry Gwin   Ridgway M. Hall

Michael Haltzel   John Harper   Stanfield Hill

Alexander Paul Hixon   Robert Jacunski   Hewitt Jeter

Philip A. Johnson   William F. Kay   Lindsey Kiang

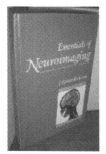

J. Robert Kirkwood   Michael E. D. Koenig   Robert Lacy

John Lahr   John Lahr   John Lahr

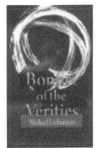  

Michael Lieberman   Thomas Lovejoy   Barry Lydgate

Stephen R. MacKinnon   Laton McCartney   Thomas McGlashan

Williamson Murray   Williamson Murray   Williamson Murray

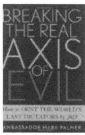
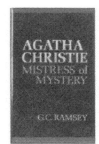

Robie Palmer   Gordon Clark Ramsey   Anthony Rhinelander

William Pennell Rock   John S. Rohsenow   David Rudenstine

John R. Sack   Brian Salzberg   Stanton Samenow

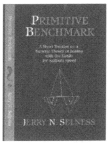

Murray Sargent III Fredric Schneider Jerry Selness

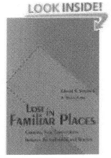

Edward R. Shapiro Harvey B. Simon Tom Stempel

Phillips Stevens, Jr.   Samuel N. Stokes   William D. Sudderth

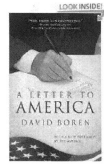

Fritz Thiel   A.O. Dennis Willows   David Boren

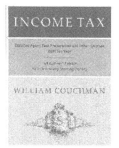
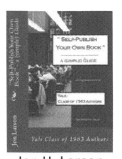

William Couchman   Jon H. Larson -   William Nordhaus
Yale Class of 1963

Douglas Allen - *The Philosophy of Mahatma Gandhi for the Twenty-First Century*

I am author and editor of 15 books including *Structure and Creativity in Religion, Culture and Self: Philosophical and Religious Perspectives, East and West*, *Myth and Religion in Mircea Eliade*, and *The Philosophy of Mahatma Gandhi for the Twenty-First Century*.

I first become interested in Gandhi during my first Fulbright year in India, 1963-1964. Gandhi's philosophy and methods shaped my personal values and involvement in the Civil Rights Movement and the Antiwar Movement. During the past 20 years, I've developed a more scholarly understanding of Gandhi and have lectured and published widely on Gandhi's philosophy and how to creatively and selectively reformulate it in ways that are relevant today. *Mahatma Gandhi*, my most recent book, is different in that it is a much shorter book and is intended to be accessible not only to scholars but also especially to motivated general readers.

Book description: Often considered the most admired human being of the twentieth century, Mahatma Gandhi was and remains controversial. Among the leading Gandhi scholars in the world, the authors of the timely studies in this volume present numerous ways in which Gandhi's thought and action-oriented approach are significant, relevant, and urgently needed for addressing the major problems and concerns of the twenty-first century.

Such problems and concerns include issues of violence and nonviolence, war and peace, religion and religious conflict and dialogue, terrorism, ethics, civil disobedience, injustice, modernism and postmodernism, forms of oppression and exploitation, and environmental destruction.

Joseph Alpert - *The Manual of Coronary Care*
and Cardiovascular Pathophysiology

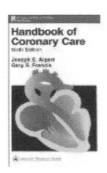 

These two books, *The Manual of Coronary Care* and *Cardiovascular Pathophysiology*, were two of my earliest books. The Manual was one of the earliest attempts at developing clinical protocols/guidelines to help physicians taking care of patients with heart attacks.

This book went through four subsequent editions and was translated into Japanese, Spanish, Chinese, and German. The second book, *Cardiovascular Pathophysiology*, was written for second year medical students studying abnormal function in various organs. This book sought to help them understand what goes wrong in the cardiovascular system when disease develops.

It leads naturally into discussions of therapy which aim at reversing the abnormal cardiovascular function. Both books were published by Little, Brown & Company, a prestigious Boston publisher with many famous authors in their "stable".

Book description: This well-organized handbook covers the newest and most important therapeutic strategies for handling medical problems that occur in the coronary care unit. It addresses everything from diet to indications for transfer to the CCU to the vital role of the CCU nurse. Ideal for cardiologists, coronary care unit nurses, house staff, or any physician with a CCU patient, this pocket guide provides practical information that is quickly accessible. Updated throughout, this new edition offers an increased emphasis on myocardial infarction and thrombolysis.

Walter G. Alton, Jr   - *Medical Malpractice,*
                              A Trial Lawyer's Advice to Physicians

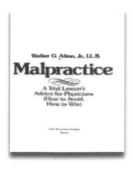

Medical Malpractice, A Trial Lawyer's Advice to Physicians, published by Little, Brown, was written by me when I was a medical malpractice defense lawyer after the successful defense of two physicians who urged me to write what I had taught them.

It consists of basic explanations of the anatomy of a medical malpractice lawsuit and advice as to how to prevent such a lawsuit and win if you are sued. The basics and principles in the book still hold true today. The irony is that I began representing injured plaintiffs and their families in 1985 and still am.

Myron Arms - *Riddle of the Ice*

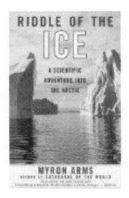

During the two decades from 1990 to 2010, I led a series of adventure-cruises aboard a 50-foot sailing cutter, *Brendan's Isle*, into the Arctic and sub-Arctic waters of the North Atlantic Ocean. *Riddle of the Ice* chronicles one of these journeys: a 6,000-mile sailing voyage from the east coast of the United States to the ice fields of Disko Bay, Greenland.

The voyage functions as the narrative vehicle for the real subject of the book: a series of conversations with key scientific investigators about changes in the Arctic sea regime and their relation to patterns of changing global climate. The book, which became a Boston Globe bestseller, was enthusiastically reviewed.

Harvard energy guru Michael McElroy stated: "I can't think of another book that makes the complexities of the global warming dialogue so accessible to the lay audience." *Riddle of the Ice* is one of four books I have published on the northern voyages of *Brendan's Isle*, and is (so far) the most successful.

Book description: By any account, the impenetrable barrier of sea ice that blocked the *Brendan's Isle* halfway up the Labrador Coast should not have been there in late July, in what was one of the hottest summers in memory a few hundred miles to the south. Frustrated and mystified at having to turn back so early in his 1991 northbound voyage, sailor Myron Arms became determined to explain the anomaly.

Jeffrey Barnouw - *Propositional Perception. Phantasia, Predication and Sign in Plato, Aristotle and the Stoics*

This book is a pendant to my *Propositional Perception. Phantasia, Predication, and Sign in Plato, Aristotle and the Stoics* (2002). The ancient Greek Stoics, particularly the great Chrysippus, were the main focus of the first book. Plato cited Homeric scenes of inward deliberation as evidence for his theory of a tri-partite soul. Chrysippus countered that interpretation as part of his rejection of the notion of an irrational faculty. Homer's scenes of deliberation do not show a "higher" rational part opposing a desiring or passionate part of the soul. Deliberation is rather the contention of opposing impulses or plans, in each of which there must a reasoned and a passionate component. This is a conception later developed by such thinkers as Thomas Hobbes and John Dewey. The middle part of the book traces the conflict of these two approaches in psychological philosophy from Plato and Chrysippus to the American Pragmatists.

Book description: The early Greek Stoics were the first philosophers to recognize the object of normal human perception as predicative or propositional in nature. Fundamentally we do not perceive qualities or things, but situations and things happening, facts. To mark their difference from Plato and Aristotle, the Stoics adopted phantasia as their word for perception. This term had been coined by Plato to designate "deceptive appearance," a combination of sensation and judgment, and the Stoics turned this sense to positive account, by linking it to the ground-breaking work of Plato and Aristotle on predication, the framing of propositions.

Michael Davitt Bell - *The Development of American Romance:*
The Sacrifice of Relation

Michael Davitt Bell earned his M.A. and Ph.D. at Harvard, and taught at Harvard and Princeton until 1975, when he joined the faculty at Williams College.

At Williams, he was J. Leland Miller Professor of American History, Literature, and Eloquence from 1981 until his untimely death from cancer in 1997, and served as Chair of the English Department from 1987 to 1994.

Richard Brodhead described him as "one of the most clear headed and generous minded contributors to the study of American literature."

He was the author of several books, which are represented here by *The Development of American Romance: The Sacrifice of Relation* (1980) and *The Problem of American Realism: Studies in the Cultural History of a Literary Idea* (1996).

F. Michler Bishop – *Managing Addictions*

The treatment of addictions was limited when I wrote this book in 2000. My goal was to write a book that reflected what we knew from research about what worked. I also wanted to make the book accessible to a wide variety of practitioners, from Ph.D. licensed psychologists to counselors working in correctional settings. With the help of a wonderful editor, the book came out better than I had hoped for. As the late Dr. Alan Marlatt, a true revolutionary in the field, wrote in the foreword, it "represents the cutting edge of the emerging paradigm shift in addiction treatment." Unfortunately, however, treatment options remain limited in this country. Research suggests more than a dozen ways to manage and, in some cases, overcome addictions, but those ways continue to be underutilized.

Book description: People who suffer from addictive disorders present an incredible challenge to therapists. This book offers hope and specific techniques designed to address the complexity of treatment. Dr. F. Michler Bishop stresses the need for therapists to be flexible, to recognize that different people have different needs, and to consider a variety of perspectives. Cognitive, emotive, behavioral, and spiritual modalities are presented with rich clinical detail.

Addressing not only substance abuse, but also shopping, eating, gambling, and sexual behaviors, the book considers such issues as assessment, denial, dual diagnosis, anxiety, shame and guilt. The change process is described in various stages and therapists are reminded that patients need to move through the process, stop the process, and even go into reverse many times before they reach their treatment goals. Of particular interest is the advice he gives on working with non-motivated patients. In contrast to the confrontational, aggressive approach that has been advocated by addictions specialists in the past, Dr. Bishop suggests that therapist confrontations increase the probability of relapse.

David Boren – *A Letter to America*

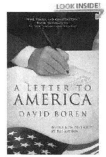

Book Description: *"A Letter to America"* boldly faces the question of how long the United States, with only six percent of the world's population, can remain a global superpower. University of Oklahoma president David Boren explains with unsparing clarity why the country is at a crossroads and why decisive action is urgently needed. He draws on his experiences as the longest-serving chair of the U.S. Senate's Select Committee on Intelligence and as a state governor and leader of a major public university.

Boren asserts major reforms to restore the ability of our political system to act responsibly. We have shared values, and we should use them to replace cynicism with hope and the determination to build a better future. Bipartisan cooperation on behalf of national interests needs to replace destructive partisanship, and we should not rule out electing a president independent of both existing parties. We must fashion a post-Cold War foreign policy that fits twenty-first-century realities--including several contending superpowers.

We must adopt campaign finance reform that restores political power to the voters, rather than special interests. Universal health care coverage, budget deficit reduction, affordable higher education, and a more progressive tax structure will strengthen the middle class.

Boren also describes how we can renew our emphasis on quality primary and secondary education, revitalize our spirit of community, and promote volunteerism. He urges the teaching of more American history and government, for without educated citizens our system cannot function and our rights will not be preserved. Unless we understand how we became great, we will not remain great.

Stephen Bradley - *Applied Mathematical Programming*

When I received my Ph.D. in Operations Research from the University of California at Berkeley, I had no intention of pursuing an academic career.

However, after a false start at IBM, I ended up on the Managerial Economics faculty at the Harvard Business School, where for the first 15 to 20 years I worked on quantitative analysis of business problems.

My book *Applied Mathematical Programming*, written with Arnoldo Hax and Tom Magnanti, all of us students of George B. Dantzig, has never been revised and is still in use today.

At Harvard Business School I had the flexibility to change my research focus and moved to the Competition and Strategy area.

My book *Sense & Respond, Capturing the Value in the Network Area*, with Richard Nolan, illustrates the type of research that I have pursued ever since moving to strategy.

L. Paul Bremer III - *My Year in Iraq: The Struggle to Build a Future of Hope* and *From Sea to Shining Sea*

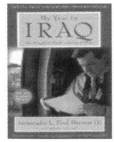

My Year in Iraq: The Struggle to Build a Future of Hope tells the story of my stormy 14 months as Presidential Envoy to Iraq after the liberation of Iraq. The setting is the first occupation undertaken by America since the Second World War. The reader learns of the enormous political, economic, and social challenges faced by thousands of civilian volunteers from 25 nations as they undertook the task of rebuilding a nation shattered by three decades of brutal tyranny. The book recounts the deleterious impact of the failure of the Coalition to provide adequate security to the Iraqi people.

Book description: "BAGHDAD WAS BURNING." With these words, Ambassador L. Paul "Jerry" Bremer begins his gripping memoir of fourteen danger-filled months as America's proconsul in Iraq. *My Year in Iraq* is the only senior insider's perspective on the crucial period following the collapse of Saddam Hussein's regime. His memoir carries the reader behind closed doors in Baghdad during hammer-and-tongs negotiations with emerging Iraqi leaders as they struggle to forge the democratic institutions vital to Iraq's future of hope. He describes his private meetings with President Bush and his admiration for the president's firm wartime leadership. And we witness heated sessions among members of America's National Security Council -- George Bush, Dick Cheney, Colin Powell, Donald Rumsfeld, and Condoleezza Rice -- as Bremer labors to realize the vision he and President Bush share of a free and democratic New Iraq. He admires the selfless and courageous work of thousands of American servicemen and -women and civilians in Iraq.

I self-published a second book, *From Sea to Shining Sea: Biking Across America with Wounded Warriors* (2011). This dramatic story tells of the remarkable challenges 16 wounded men and women faced during a two month 4,000 mile bike ride from San Francisco's Bay Bridge to Virginia Beach. Riding with the wounded warriors, I recount how the people of America—in small towns, farm communities and big cities—came out to thank these brave men and women for their service to our country.

Judson W. "Jud" Calkins - *Teammates for Life*

In an eight-year career with the St. Louis Post-Dispatch, I chronicled significant events of the 1960s and '70s, but my first book came only in 2012, after my alma mater John Burroughs School in St. Louis invited me to write the rich athletic history of the school in co-authorship with Jim Lemen, the outgoing Burroughs athletic director and Dartmouth football captain, '62, against whom I had competed in the Yale Bowl.

A year and a half of research and interviews led to *Teammates for Life*, a 267-page work replete with photographs, images, narrative text, and feature stories recounting 90 years of competition in a host of sports, often involving Burroughs as private school Davids slaying public school Goliaths.

The book covers Missouri state championships claimed in abundance, courage and sportsmanship displayed on the field, and important personal values gleaned along the way.

Charles C. Cheney - *Biomedical Globalization:*

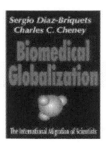

Biomedical Globalization: The International Migration of Scientists (2002), written with Sergio Díaz-Briquets, is a study of the employment of foreign biomedical scientists as post-doctoral fellows by the National Institutes of Health in Bethesda, Maryland. We found that NIH's post-doctoral programs are, as designed, more complementary than competitive, and that after American and foreign scientists have worked together at NIH and the latter have subsequently returned home, they often continue to communicate and collaborate long-distance in pursuing their respective biomedical research endeavors.

Book description: Despite much debate in recent years about the economic and professional impact of foreign engineers and computer professionals in the United States, comparatively little has been said about the growing number of foreign biomedical scientists employed by American firms and health institutions. The implications are widespread and merit serious analysis. In *Biomedical Globalization*, Diaz-Briquets and Cheney shed light on this development through examination of the experience of foreign biomedical scientists at the National Institutes of Health (NIH) in Bethesda, Maryland.

Diaz-Briquets and Cheney's analysis is based on results of ethnographic field observations and more than 200 interviews among diverse biomedical research constituencies in the United States and abroad. These views provide a penetrating glimpse into the complex web of interrelationships governing the international mobility of highly skilled personnel within a given scientific field. While the work of the NIH is unexceptionable in advancing biomedical knowledge and forging international research linkages, a far more complex and elusive picture emerges when the issue is placed within a broader labor market perspective. Under some circumstances the United States economy may suffer from the presence of foreign biomedical scientists in American laboratories.

Biomedical Globalization will be of interest to policymakers, labor studies scholars, and scientific researchers.

Clifford Clark - *The American Family Home* and *The Enduring Vision*

When I began my book, *The American Family Home, 1800-1960* (1986), I wanted to know why middle-class Americans, in cities, suburbs, and small towns, spent so much time and energy fixing and remodeling their homes. Why were these homes, which seemed so stylistically similar, treasured as symbols of independence and personal identity? How did the house get so closely associated with the ideal of the family? Why has house remodeling produced such popular television shows? And most importantly, was there any connection between the popular ideals of home and family as expressed in advice books, magazines, and pattern books, and the actual relationship between individual houses and the families who lived in them?

In producing this book, I was fortunate to have a talented friend, Richard Hendel, one of the leading book designers in the U.S., who worked at the book's layout and illustrations. The University of North Carolina Press had a strong American History section, and also provided helpful editorial suggestions.

My section of *The Enduring Vision* textbook covers late nineteenth century politics, social and intellectual history, and popular culture.

All self-publishers should also think carefully about the issues of book layout, design, and illustrations. (See Richard Hendel, *On Book Design* (1998).

Bud Conrad – *Profiting from the World's Economic Crisis*

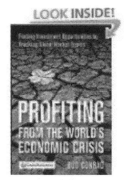

Book description: In *Profiting from the World's Economic Crisis,* author Bud Conrad, Chief Economist for Casey Research, predicts a rough road ahead for us—due to economic imbalances that have built up over the past decade—but reveals how you can prosper during these difficult times by tracking global market trends and finding investment opportunities that match those trends.

With this book, Conrad outlines the long-term direction of our economy as driven by increasing U.S. government and trade deficits, oil prices, Social Security and Medicare obligations for baby boomers, the credit crisis, and the weakening dollar. He also examines why some of the government's actions—such as bailing out banks and curbing interest rates—fail to address more serious, long-term issues such as too much debt.

The crisis we have entered is not a typical business recession, but, instead, a major deleveraging which is the biggest shift since the Great Depression. The stagflation of the U.S. economy will present great challenges on a global scale. And since no market travels in a straight line, you need to be positioned correctly, with the right investments, to protect yourself and to profit from the twists and turns you'll inevitably face in today's turbulent economic environment.

Bud Conrad has been a futures investor for twenty-five years as well as a full-time investor for more than a decade. He holds an MBA from Harvard and an electrical engineering degree from Yale. Conrad has held positions with IBM, CDC, Amdahl, and Tandem. His comprehensive picture of the world's economy, based on a career of using long-term fundamental analysis, enables him to explain how this crisis arose and where it will evolve. He uses insights learned from his engineering training to interpret how investment cycles affect our economy.

Donald Cooke - *Fun with GPS*

Fun with GPS came out of my professional use of the Global Positioning System at Geographic Data Technology, Inc. and years of school and community outreach based on using GPS and GIS (Geographic Information System) technology in classrooms, science fair projects, town planning and conservation.

I was frustrated by the perception that thousands of people were buying GPS units (not the car navigation devices) and simply using them for Geocaching. (*Geocaching* is a treasure hunting game where you use a GPS to hide and seek containers with other participants in the activity). While I have nothing against Geocaching, I saw these devices as precision sensor/storage units that opened up worlds of mapping and data analysis.

So the book consists of thirty illustrated "stunts" involving attaching GPS units to skydivers, skiers, pet animals – even a wild bear – then mapping their travels. Plus I couldn't resist adding some nerdy semi-scientific observations from the entire exercise.

Many thanks to Jack and Laura Dangermond, founders of ESRI, for sponsoring and publishing the book.

David Bruce Cornay - *Eros and Nihilism:*
Studies in the Possibility of a Human World

Bruce Cornay earned his M.A. from Tulane University in 1970, and his Ph.D. in 1974. In 1976, with Charles Bigger, he published *Eros and Nihilism: Studies in the Possibility of a Human World*, a collection of essays and readings constituting an introduction to philosophy.

As described in the preface to the book, Eros "is the theme of the dynamics of human need and our efforts to achieve conditions for satisfaction transcending the immediate now," while Nihilism sees this goal as beyond attainment.

In his later life, Bruce was Chairman of Cornay Web Graphics, Inc., and served as the Chairman of the Louisiana Capital Area Health Planning Commission Committee on Drug Abuse and as a Board member of the Baton Rouge Alcohol and Drug Acute Treatment Center.

Book description: It remains a noteworthy accomplishment that reflects the uncertain shift from modernism to post-modernism occurring at that time. The theme of the text, *Eros and Nihilism*, focuses on the two main opposing forces in human existence--the erotic, creative force behind our construction of a world, versus the nihilistic, destructive force directed toward nothingness.

Thus, the text juxtaposes selections from Plato, Nietzsche, Freud, Feuerbach and others, with insightful commentaries written by several members of the LSU philosophy faculty, including Charles Bigger, David Cornay (deceased), Edward Shirley (deceased) and Kenneth Smith, who also created the cover

William Couchman - *Income Tax:*
                       Enrolled Agent Test Preparation and Other Topics

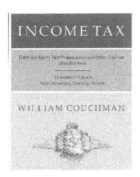

I have written *Income Tax: Enrolled Agent Test Preparation and Other Topics* as the primary material for tax courses I teach. The first three chapters, entitled Enrolled Agent Test Preparation – Parts I, II, and III, are to prepare experienced tax professionals to pass the three IRS Special Enrollment Exams to become Enrolled Agents (essentially a CPA-level IRS certification specializing in taxes).

I have taught this course for five years at H&R Block and as Adjunct Instructor at Northwestern University. The fourth chapter, entitled All-States Class, covers tax regulations in the states surrounding Illinois, for tax preparers familiar mostly with Illinois regulations.

The fifth chapter, entitled Commonly Missed Tax Savings Opportunities, Second Looks, and Amended Returns, teaches the savings to look for and the mechanics of doing amended returns. I have taught the latter two courses to 200 students.

Richard Bates Couser - *The Deuteronomy Project:*
                              A Journey into the Mind of God

After Yale, Dick Couser studied law at Stanford, where he was on the Law Review. He practiced all of his career in Concord, New Hampshire, distinguishing himself as a business lawyer and earning a reputation for integrity and diligence. Later in life, he experienced a calling to Christianity. In 1993, he wrote his first book, *Ministry and the American Legal System.*

In 2008, his second book, *The Deuteronomy Project: A Journey into the Mind of God,* was published. The Deuteronomy Project includes the entire text of the Book of Deuteronomy for reading and reflection, telling the story and explaining the Scripture in a way lay Christians can understand, and relating the text to the teachings of Jesus and New Testament writers.

Book description: "*The Deuteronomy Project*" by Richard B. Couser is an incredibly creative Bible study imbedded in a beautiful story. Don't allow yourself to be dissuaded from picking up this rather imposing book. The sheer size of it is enough to intimidate the most voracious reader of Christian fiction or intense student of scripture. If you give this book even half a chance, you will come away from the experience enriched!

Not only is there an intricately woven story, the entire text of the book of Deuteronomy is contained within the pages. There is a set of discussion/study questions in the back of the book that will assist in maximizing the benefits of learning Biblical truth from this fictional text. This book is a wonderful way to broaden your knowledge of Deuteronomy and how to study scripture, in general. "*The Deuteronomy Project*" belongs in every Bible student's library!

Leo Damrosch - *Jonathan Swift: His Life and His World*

After three decades of writing monographs for the tiny audience of fellow specialists in 18th century literature, I made my breakaway in 2005 with my first "trade press" book, *Jean-Jacques Rousseau: Restless Genius*. There was no single-volume biography of Rousseau in English, and the three-volume standard biography glossed over most of what made Rousseau a complicated personality and – despite having no formal education whatsoever – an astonishingly original thinker. The book did well and was nominated for the National Book Award in nonfiction. Five years later I drew on my French interest for Tocqueville's *Discovery of America*, an account of the remarkable journey the 25 year old Tocqueville he made throughout the U.S. in 1831-32. He met John Quincy Adams in Boston, Andrew Jackson in the White House, and Sam Houston on a Mississippi riverboat, and along the way he developed the ideas that would bear fruit in Democracy in America. My latest book, *Jonathan Swift: His Life and His World* was published in 2013 by Yale University Press, and won the National Book Critics Circle award for biography.

Book description: Jonathan Swift is best remembered today as the author of Gulliver's Travels, the satiric fantasy that quickly became a classic and has remained in print for nearly three centuries. Yet Swift also wrote many other influential works, was a major political and religious figure in his time, and became a national hero, beloved for his fierce protest against English exploitation of his native Ireland.

In this deeply researched biography, Leo Damrosch draws on discoveries made over the past thirty years to tell the story of Swift's life anew. Probing holes in the existing evidence, he takes seriously some daring speculations about Swift's parentage, love life, and various personal relationships and shows how Swift's public version of his life—the one accepted until recently—was deliberately misleading.

Through his own words and those of a wide circle of friends, a complex Swift emerges: a restless, combative, empathetic figure, a man of biting wit and powerful mind, and a major figure in the history of world letters.

Edward A. Dennis - *Cell Signaling Collection*

  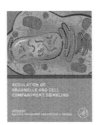 

The Cell Signaling Collection comprises four thematic volumes with the most up-to-date research on cell signaling systems:

I.	Functioning of Transmembrane Receptors in Cell Signaling
II.	Transduction Mechanisms in Cellular Signaling
III.	Regulation of Organelle and Cell Compartment Signaling
IV.	Intercellular Signaling in Development and Disease

Cell signaling mechanisms are researched and studied in graduate programs in cell biology, molecular biology, biochemistry, pharmacology, molecular and cellular physiology, and biomedical sciences. These volumes are meant for graduate students and academic and industrial researchers.

Book description: A primary component of cell signaling research, this title covers the principal membrane-bound receptor families, including their structural organization. Written and edited by experts in the field, this book provides up-to-date research on trans-membrane signaling entities and their initiating responses following extracellular stimulation.

Robert B. Dickie - *Financial Statement Analysis*
and Business Valuation for the Practical Lawyer
Corporations and the Common Good

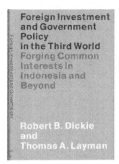

Bob Dickie is a Principal of The Dickie Group, which has earned a national and international reputation at the point of convergence among corporate law, finance, and strategy. His fourth book, *Financial Statement Analysis and Business Valuation for the Practical Lawyer*, was published by the American Bar Association and was its best seller for 1999 (2d edition 2006).

Written expressly for business lawyers, this best-selling book arms the reader with a practical working knowledge of the skills needed to navigate financial statements, the key metrics for assessing performance and prospects, and the major methods of valuing companies.

Previously, Bob was a tenured Professor at the Boston University School of Management, where his books included (1) *Corporations and the Common Good*, University of Notre Dame Press, 1986, edited with Leroy S. Rouner, and (2) *Foreign Investment and Government Policy in the Third World: Forging Common Interests in Indonesia and Beyond*, McMillan's Press in the U.K and St. Martin's Press in the U.S., 1988, co-authored with Thomas A. Layman. The former was a series of essays authored by leading corporate leaders and academics, including Ted Murray (Yale '63), on the role of the corporation in modern society. The latter assessed the dynamic tension in the third world between multinational corporations and host governments and provided counsel, some later applied by the World Bank, regarding the laws, policies, and institutional infrastructure needed to attract foreign capital, keep domestic savings at home, and harness foreign capital and know-how to build host country economies.

Anthony Elson - *Globalization and Development: Why East Asia Surged Ahead and Latin America Fell Behind* and *Governing Global Finance*

 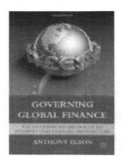

Globalization and Development: Why East Asia Surged Ahead and Latin America Fell Behind. Since the middle of the last century, East Asia and Latin America have followed very different development trajectories, with East Asia rapidly increasing its income per capita in relation to that of the US, while Latin America has fallen steadily behind. This book attempts to explain this divergent outcome by identifying the historical, institutional, and political economy factors that can account for the different economic policy choices that governments in the two regions have made. To a large extent, this book represents the distillation of my thinking about these issues for many years as an academic and professional economist

Governing Global Finance, deals with the international arrangements that governments have put in place to safeguard the operations of the global financial system, which have come to be known as the international financial architecture (IFA). The principal organizations involved in the IFA are the International Monetary Fund, the Bank for International Settlements, the Financial Stability Board, and the G20.

The first part of the book explains how the IFA has evolved since the end of World War II, largely in response to crises associated with the growth of financial globalization.

The latter part of the book deals with the causes of the global financial crisis that erupted in 2007-08, the international response via the IFA, and the ongoing debate about how to reform the IFA in the wake of the recent crisis.

Norman Etherington - *Oxford History of the British Empire*

As a Yale undergraduate and graduate student, my aspiration as a writer was to one day have my name in gold letters on the spine of a book that would stand for decades on the shelves of libraries around the world. An invitation to become one of the editors of the *Oxford History of the British Empire* fulfilled that dream.

When I undertook the commission in 1999, I had no idea of the hours, weeks and months it would take to assemble a team of experts and whip the final volume into shape. This book emerged from a long process of consultation, including symposia in Switzerland and Australia.

Even after all that effort, in order to meet the word limit, I had personally to impose line by line cuts on authors who insisted that not a single word could go. The reviews and sales have made it all worthwhile.

Book description: The widespread idea that Christian missions went hand in hand with Imperialism and colonial conquest is challenged here by a group of eminent historians. By showing the variety of missions and the vital role played by indigenous men and women, they place missions in a long historical perspective. Special attention is paid to emerging themes such as the missionary role in anthropology, gender relations, language, medicine, and decolonization.

Carter V. Findley – *Turkey, Islam, Nationalism, and Modernity: A History, 1789-2007*

The summer after I graduated from Yale I came upon a book that looked important for my chosen field of graduate study. The book was Bernard Lewis' *Emergence of Modern Turkey* (1961). I bought it. As I started reading my shiny new book, I began to ask myself, "What would it take to write a book like that?" By the time I finished reading Bernard's book, I also thought it was not as well organized or tied together thematically as it could have been.

Excellent use of primary sources, but too much reliance on writing style instead of structural integration. As time went by, I started asking what it would take to write a book that covered the same subject matter, brought it up to date, and was well tied together thematically and analytically. It took a while to come up with my best answer to that question. How nice for me that Yale University Press noticed it and published it. Its Turkish translation is also doing well in Turkey.

Robert J. Flanagan - *The Perilous Life of Symphony Orchestras*

This book explores the paradox that while symphonic music has probably never been performed at a higher level, most symphony orchestras are living on the edge financially. The book demonstrates how the economic jeopardy facing many orchestras (and other performing arts organizations) is rooted in the limited opportunities for increasing productivity in the arts, a situation that produces ongoing cost pressures and structural budget deficits. A decline in the demand for classical music performances (and for most performing arts) exacerbates the jeopardy.

The book also contrasts the experience of orchestras in the United States (where there is little direct government support for the performing arts) and abroad (where governments typically provide large direct subsidies).

Finally, the book analyzes three complementary strategies for addressing orchestras' economic challenges—raising performance revenues, slowing the growth of performance expenses, and increasing non-performance income—and demonstrates that none of the three strategies *alone* is likely to provide economic security for orchestras.

Richard N. Foster - *Innovation: The Attacker's Advantage*
and
Creative Destruction: Why Companies That Are Built to Last Underperform the Market--and How to Successfully Transform Them

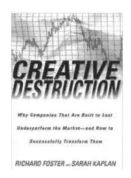

Having completed my B.S. in Chemical Engineering at Yale in 1963, I was surprised to find myself in the Yale Ph.D. program for Engineering and Applied Science. The Ph.D. was awarded in 1966 and I was off to the working life of a young working graduate. Almost nothing I found working had been anticipated in my education. Broad questions about the utility of technological advance that had not been addressed in my education became clear and important to me.

I reflected on these issues for about two decades and then published my first book (*Innovation: The Attacker's Advantage*) on the topic. I was surprised when it became a global best seller and translated into 16 languages. There were still, however, unanswered questions, particularly about the role of the global capital markets in encouraging or discouraging technological advance.

I wrote about that in 2001 with *Creative Destruction: Why Companies That Are Built to Last Underperform the Market--and How to Successfully Transform Them,* and was fortunate enough to have another best seller. My final surprise (so far!) was when the Harvard Business Review cited my books as among the "Great Moments in Management" in the past century.

For the last ten years I have continued to explore the capital market and managerial implications of technological change not only in the US but abroad — China, Latin America, Europe (and particularly Eastern Europe) and gradually Africa.

Richard Friedlander - *Paradise Besieged*

"Why in hell should I care about men who think it is a holy act to give up meat, never wash, and abstain from women and every other form of human intercourse?" That has to be the first question asked by anyone confronting *Paradise Besieged* and unfamiliar with its subject. Relax, you are not alone.

This book is a spiritual journey only as it reveals the humanity of the monks among whom I spent many years, and is odds-on to offend those who are secure in their possession of the One and Only Truth. Change is what this book is really about: the clash of irresistible forces, immovable objects, temporality, and eternity, the tensions without which there is no life. To my chagrin, *Paradise Besieged* has actually been praised by clergy; to my pleasure and astonishment, its surprisingly broad audience has included many women.

Book description: Richard John Friedlander, mediator, church ecclesiarch, and Greek Orthodox Christian agnostic Jew, takes you on a decidedly unorthodox journey to the Holy Mountain of Athos in Greece—a wondrous and wild land where the only residents are monks and no one used the word "change" for over a thousand years.

Born in Brooklyn, a graduate of Yale and Yale Law School, Friedlander became a Greek Orthodox Christian at the Christ-like age of thirty-three and lived for the better part of the next ten years in this outpost of the Middle Ages like a Yankee in the Mother of God's Court, becoming intimately familiar with the beauty, rigors, and absurdities of monastic life, and learning how to survive, and even thrive, without modernity.

Michael Gates Gill - *How Starbucks Saved My Life:*
A Son of Privilege Learns to Live Like Everyone Else

After I was fired from my job, got divorced, and was diagnosed with a brain tumor, I was spiraling down in a vortex of increasing guilt, depression and a sense that my life was over. At that point my daughter Annie suggested that I begin keeping a journal. Reading the journal twelve months after having begun to work as a barista at Starbucks I realized that my former guilt and depression had been replaced with a surprising kind of happiness I had never known before.

I thought then that sharing my experience might help others when they encountered terrible and unforeseen shocks. Telling my truth that was full of humiliations as well as new learning experiences was not an easy challenge – especially for a former Yale Man and advertising guy. But I found that through writing the book, and telling this truth, it helped me to heal the past and share the unexpected gift of the joy I found in my new life. My book has now been translated into over 20 languages and I am grateful to hear that my story has helped others to create lives they love.

Book description: ... the national bestselling riches-to-rags true story of an advertising executive who had it all, then lost it all—and was finally redeemed by his new job, and his twenty-eight-year-old boss, at Starbucks.

In his fifties, Michael Gates Gill had it all: a mansion in the suburbs, a wife and loving children, a six-figure salary, and an Ivy League education. But in a few short years, he lost his job, got divorced, and was diagnosed with a brain tumor. With no money or health insurance, he was forced to get a job at Starbucks. Having gone from power lunches to scrubbing toilets, from being served to serving, Michael was a true fish out of water. But fate brings an unexpected teacher into his life who opens his eyes to what living well really looks like. The two seem to have nothing in common: She is a young African American, the daughter of a drug addict; he is used to being the boss but reports to her now. For the first time in his life he experiences being a member of a minority trying hard to survive in a challenging new job.

Art Gilliam – *One America: Moving Beyond the Issue of Race*

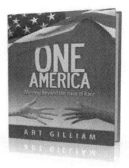

I remember that short bus ride in Memphis, my home town. It was a few years before Rosa Parks refused to sit in the back of a Montgomery, Alabama bus and triggered a bus boycott by Negroes, which was the initial incident that brought that boycott's leader, Martin Luther King, to the nation's attention. But that would all come later. I was only thinking about the arts and crafts awaiting me at Bethlehem Center and how proud I was that my mom trusted me to ride the bus alone. It meant I was a "big boy"!

If I had written a book proposal back then about what happened to that boy, it would have had the most improbable of story lines. He would leave the segregated South at thirteen to attend a nearly all-white New England prep school and seven years later would graduate from Yale University. He would earn a master's degree in actuarial science and go on later to buy a radio station in Memphis. Eventually, he would marry a white girl living in Copenhagen, Denmark and together in Memphis they would watch a fellow named Barack Hussein Obama, who has an African father and a white American mother, be sworn in as President of the United States. Even the most liberal of book proposal reviewers would have relegated that one to the fantasyland bin. That is, if the script and author made it past the nearest insane asylum, assuming the author was not lynched before having the opportunity to be committed. Yet here we are only a few decades later, and the story is in the category of nonfiction. I suppose it would be fair to say this could only happen in America.

Book description: The author shares his experience of growing up in the Deep South in the 1950's – a time when racism was pervasive. His personal story reflects the impact on the black psyche of being black in America during the transition from the back of the bus to the election of a black president. Art's education at a New England prep school and Yale University led to a compelling change in his perspective. He shares the insights he gained about the critical differences between the self images of blacks and whites and how this influences our perceptions of each other.

Gerard Gold -
Business and Higher Education: Toward New Alliances

Business and Higher Education: Toward New Alliances developed from national demonstration projects in the 1970s for the non-profit National Institute for Work and Learning. For the U.S. Department of Education, I'd directed a project documenting varieties of community-based education-work collaborative councils.

Some of these councils began to show how better communication and institutional commitments among community leaders, especially local employers and secondary schools and community colleges, could address problems of school-to-work transition, local economic development, and technological and social change.

Aware of these projects, the Council for the Advancement of Learning asked me to invite authors who examined relationships between higher education and employment institutions from multiple points of view, looking to new forms of collaboration.

Donald Avery Graham -
> *Complete Works of Pir-O-Murshid Hazrat Inayat Khan*

After an academic career of 30 years in Arizona, I was invited to become editor-in-chief of the *Complete Works of Pir-O-Murshid Hazrat Inayat Khan* in Suresnes, France, a suburb of Paris. I worked there from 1998 through 2012.

Inayat Khan was an Indian musician and Sufi spiritual teacher who came to the West in 1910 (the first Sufi teacher to do so) and lived in Paris from 1950 to 1957, when he died. We have now published eleven volumes of his lectures and sayings. The complete series will be sixteen or seventeen volumes.

It is a scholarly edition, in which we have returned to the most original sources, in many cases shorthand taken down as Inayat Khan was speaking. He has been widely published, but in a highly edited form that often is quite different from what he actually said. This edition returns to his actual words, so far as that can be ascertained, and footnotes the variations in other manuscripts and in early publications. It is not intended for casual reading, but to form the basis of future editions staying close to Inayat Khan's actual words.

Publication was arranged with a small publishing house, Omega Press of New Lebanon, New York, with the Dutch foundation which supervises the archive providing funds which are paid back as the books sell. About equal numbers of the books have sold in the United States and Europe, with further sales in India.

Thomas S. Greenspon - *Moving Past Perfect:*
How Perfectionism May Be Holding Back
Your Kids (and You!) and What You Can Do About It

Moving Past Perfect is an update of my book, Freeing Our Families From Perfectionism. It's for parents and teachers who are interested in ways to help young people get beyond perfectionism. Perfectionism is a desire to be perfect (not "almost perfect"), a fear of imperfection, and an emotional conviction that perfection is the route to personal acceptability. For perfectionists mistakes are signs of personal flaws, and the anxiety about making mistakes is a constant burden which interferes with personal serenity and relationship harmony, and, ironically, with performance and personal achievement.

Moving Past Perfect helps readers learn how to create an environment of acceptance, as an antidote to the self-esteem depredations that are the hallmark of perfectionism. What to Do When Good Enough Isn't Good Enough is written for middle schoolers, and is best when read along with caring adults.

Book description: Perfectionism is not about doing our best. It's not about the struggle for excellence or the healthy striving for high goals. Perfectionism is about believing that if we can just do something perfectly, other people will love and accept us—and if we can't, we'll never be good enough. That belief is a burden that can negatively affect all areas of a person's life. Fortunately, parents who recognize perfectionistic patterns in themselves, in their kids, or in their families as a whole can make positive changes that will enrich their children's lives and their own.

In this positive, practical book, psychologist Tom Greenspon explains perfectionism, where it comes from, and what parents can do about it. He describes a healing process for transforming perfectionism into healthy living practices and self-acceptance. Parents who want to help their kids move past perfectionism and live happier, healthier lives in which they're free to make mistakes, to learn, and to grow will benefit from this book.

DuPont Guerry - *Melanoma: Prevention, Detection, and Treatment*

Melanoma is an ever more common skin cancer that is readily recognized (it is most often darkly colored and distinctive in form) by our keenest sense – sight. When found in its early evolution, it is nearly invariably cured with simple, inexpensive, cosmetically uncomplicated, outpatient surgery. When discovered late, it is too commonly lethal. *Melanoma: Prevention, Detection, and Treatment,* published by Yale University Press and now in its second edition, is a collaboration between a patient, Catherine Poole, and her doctor.

We wrote it for patients, their families, and the public as an accessible and practical guide to addressing melanoma in all its manifestations. Its aims are to prevent, to detect early and cure, to manage the not yet curable, and to palliate physical and spiritual morbidities. It also attempts to make sense of the disease by touching on the biological phenomena that underlie it.

Book description: The incidence of melanoma has increased by 2000% since 1930, and one person dies each hour from the disease. This cutting-edge guide provides scientifically accurate information patients and their families need in order to understand melanoma and its treatment and to receive vital reassurance. It is also a resource for those who want information about preventing the disease or finding it early when it is most curable. Catherine M. Poole, a melanoma survivor and melanoma patient advocate for many national organizations, and Dr. DuPont Guerry, an internationally renowned melanoma expert, have collaborated to provide current, correct, and easily understood information on the disease.

Larry Gwin - *Baptism: A Vietnam Memoir*

Baptism: A Vietnam Memoir
has been in print since publication and has, to date, sold more than 52,000 copies. It chronicles my year as an infantry officer in Vietnam from July, '65, to July, '66. Author and military historian John McManus has described it as "one of the great Vietnam combat memoirs."

Book description: "The 2nd Battalion of the 7th Cavalry had the dubious distinction of being the unit that had fought the biggest battle of the war to date, and had suffered the worst casualties. We and the 1st Battalion."

A Yale graduate who volunteered to serve his country, Larry Gwin was only twenty-three years old when he arrived in Vietnam in 1965. After a brief stint in the Delta, Gwin was reassigned to the 1st Cavalry Division (Airmobile) in An Khe. There, in the hotly contested Central Highlands, he served almost nine months as executive officer for Alpha Company, 2/7, fighting against crack NVA troops in some of the war's most horrific battles.

The bloodiest conflict of all began November 12, 1965, after 2nd Battalion was flown into the Ia Drang Valley west of Pleiku. Acting as point, Alpha Company spearheaded the battalion's march to landing zone Albany for pickup, not knowing they were walking into the killing zone of an NVA ambush that would cost them 70 percent casualties.

Gwin spares no one, including himself, in his gut-wrenching account of the agony of war. Through the stench of death and the acrid smell of napalm, he chronicles the Vietnam War in all its nightmarish horror.

Ridgway M. Hall, Jr. – *All About Environmental Auditing*
and RCRA Hazardous Wastes Handbook

LOOK INSIDE!

Over the past 40 years of practicing environmental law, I have written dozens of articles, a couple of books (mostly published in limited editions by specialty publishers targeting the environmental professional audience), and a number of conference and course manuals. My most widely known book is *All About Environmental Auditing.* This book provides guidance to companies conducting an audit of their environmental compliance and possible liability exposures. It discusses how to plan and conduct an audit, the applicable laws and regulations, the means of maintaining confidentiality, and the analysis and successful use of the information resulting from the audit.

The *RCRA Hazardous Wastes Handbook* examines the latest regulatory and judicial developments involving the Resource Conservation and Recovery Act (RCRA) and provides a clear, practical explanation of its requirements. Issues addressed in this edition include the new provisions regarding recycling, the corrective action program, and the regulation of combustion units; changes in enforcement policy, civil and criminal liability, and citizen suits; and regulations regarding land disposal, underground storage tanks, facilities silting, and municipal solid waste management.

Book description: *RCRA Hazardous Wastes Handbook* examines the latest regulatory and judicial developments involving the Resource Conservation and Recovery Act (RCRA) and provides a clear, practical explanation of its requirements.   Using this book, you will learn how to manage the "field side" of RCRA compliance, including identifying hazardous waste, transporting hazardous materials under EPA and DOT regulations, and disposing of solid wastes. You will also learn how to manage the "paperwork side" of RCRA compliance, working with such documents as RCRA permits, manifests and land ban documents, and underground-storage-tank notices.

Michael Haltzel – _Between the Blocs:_
Problems & Prospects   For Europe's Neutral & Nonaligned States,
and   _The Global Ramifications of the French Revolution_

"Between the Blocs:" Problems & Prospects for Europe's Neutral & Nonaligned States" Book description: Neutrality is no longer an easily defined, static legal concept, but an evolving political practice. In this book, many of the preeminent scholars and political figures who have crafted the shape and meaning of the modern policy of neutrality in their own countries examine the theoretical and practical problems of neutrality and nonalignment in contemporary Europe.

Specific issues examined include the credibility of the security policies and military defenses of the Neutrals; the new challenges of international economic and technological interdependence pushing the Neutrals into closer cooperation with the European Community; and the role of public opinion in supporting policies of neutrality.

"Global Ramifications of the French Revolution". This collection of essays is the first to examine the impact of the French Revolution. The legacy of the French Revolution extends far beyond the borders of France or even Europe- the ramifications of the Revolution of 1789 are truly global and continue to have an impact today. Although the French Revolution was a response to purely domestic concerns, it was immediately noted at the time by observers and many participants that its ideals were universal in scope and that its message traveled well. As a model for both discourse and action, it helped usher in a new age, one we still live in today, of nationalism, constitutional government, mass politics, citizen armies, and popular sovereignty. Twelve authorities analyze the historical and ongoing impact of the French Revolution on American political culture, nationalism and freedom in Eastern Europe, Russian intellectual life, colonial bondage, Middle East politics, the Mexican Revolution, and Chinese socialism.

John Harper - *Secondary Cohomology Operations*

The book develops the theory of secondary cohomology operations in terms of elementary constructions in general homotopy theory. Cohomology is a method for attaching algebraic invariants to topological spaces. The algebraic structures that emerge can serve to distinguish spaces, especially in high dimensions. The book is intended for graduate students and research mathematicians interested in algebraic topology.

Book description: Although the theory and applications of secondary cohomology operations are an important part of an advanced graduate-level algebraic topology course, there are few books on the subject. The AMS fills that gap with the publication of the present volume.

The author's main purpose in this book is to develop the theory of secondary cohomology operations for singular cohomology theory, which is treated in terms of elementary constructions from general homotopy theory. Among many applications considered are the Hopf invariant one theorem (for all primes p, including $p = 2$), Browder's theorem on higher Bockstein operations, and cohomology theory of Massey-Peterson fibrations.

Numerous examples and exercises help readers to gain a working knowledge of the theory. A summary of more advanced parts of the core material is included in the first chapter. Prerequisite is basic algebraic topology, including the Steenrod operations. The book is geared toward graduate students and research mathematicians interested in algebraic topology and can be used for self-study or as a textbook for an advanced course on the topic.

Stanfield Hill - *Plan Smart, Retire Rich*

As a member for many years of a team of fellow attorneys in the marketing department of Mutual of New York (now part of AXA-Equitable), I enjoyed teaching agents and counseling their clients with a variety of tax saving and investment ideas, as well as estate and business planning devices.

We decided to publish some of the more popular arrangements in Smart Assets, which generated a sequel, *Plan Smart, Retire Rich*. (As a co-author, it was a lot of fun promoting these at a Barnes & Noble book signing gig in NYC.) In an earlier effort, I added a chapter on "split- dollar" life insurance to the book Business Insurance Agreements, which was given to clients' counsel as a guideline for drafting documents.

Book description: Today's changing social fabric means more Americans than ever are responsible for their own retirement security. *Plan Smart, Retire Rich* helps take the mystery out of retirement planning with profiles that readers can match to their personal goals, needs, and resources.

This hands-on guide -- from the retirement experts at MONY -- leads the reader through the creation of a powerful, personal financial plan. Guidelines to leverage the power of one's assets and resources include:
-- A comprehensive range of retirement plans and techniques
-- Strategies to turn a 401(k) into a wealth-building vehicle
-- Common mistakes many investors make, and ways to avoid them

Alexander Paul "Lex" Hixon, Jr. - *Coming Home: The Experience of Enlightenment in Sacred Traditions*

The trajectory of Lex Hixon's adult life was set in motion by a book he read as part of a Comparative Religion course during his senior year at Yale, about an Indian saint who taught that all the major religious traditions are true. For 30 years Lex traveled the globe making first-hand explorations of various initiatory lineages, always maintaining the clear and balanced overview expressed in his first book, *Coming Home: The Experience of Enlightenment in Sacred Traditions*.

Lex studied with sufis beginning in 1980, participated in the Hajj, and wrote about these experiences in The Heart of the Qur'an and other writings. He also participated in and wrote about Tibetan Buddhism and the Divine Mother Tradition of Bengal. When Lex became ill in 1995, he was preparing to go to Japan to be installed as a teacher of Zen Buddhism. Instead, he worked to finish the book Living Buddha Zen, about the studies he had undergone to become a Zen teacher.

Book description: Hixon provides a somewhat idiosyncratic yet fascinating and informative view of ten paths to enlightenment, moving from the contemplative views of Heidegger and Krishnamurti through the tantrism of Ramakrishna and the naturalism of Ramana Maharishi to the Zen ox-herding pictures, Mother Serena (a contemporary Rosicrucian teacher), the Hasidic masters, and Paul of Tarsus seen as a mystic announcing the new age of divine-human union. Included are Hixon's consultations of the I Ching and an explication of Turiya as taught by Advaita Vedanta and experienced by Hixon with Swami Nikhilananda as his teacher.

Robert Jacunski - _Quandary_

Robert Jacunski played end on the 1959 undefeated Yale freshman football team and on the 1960 undefeated Yale football team. He then transferred to Marquette University, where he earned a degree in English. He worked for the New Haven Register and for the Southern New England Telephone Company. In 2007 he published a novel, _Quandary_, about a mysterious outbreak of impotence in a Kansas farming community. The novel explores the various reactions of people to impotence, and how the choices they make affect many lives.

Book description: It's 1968 and sexual freedom is in vogue when a sudden outbreak of impotence strikes a Kansas farming community. Dr. Charles Winston and town leaders are soon afflicted and in a quandary. They feel powerless as frustration and depression spread, tragedy strikes and violence erupts.

The doctor fears that the local epidemic, if unchecked, will spread and eventually end the human race. This fascinating first novel candidly explores the reactions of people to impotence and how the choices they make affect many lives.

Quandary appeals to mature readers who enjoy a fast-paced mélange of humor, mystery, romance, religion, and psychology.

Hewitt Jeter - *A Modeling Study of Gaseous Rn-222, Xe-133,*
and He-4 for Uranium Exploration

A Modeling Study of Gaseous Rn-222, Xe-133, and He-4 for Uranium Exploration was developed under contract for the United States Department of Energy, and published in 1980 as part of a national program to evaluate uranium resources.

The study is a mathematical simulation of the dispersion of gaseous decay products away from a uranium deposit in order to determine whether the deposit could be detected remotely by analyzing these decay products in overlying soil or rock layers.

I was assigned this research project while I was the manager of a radiochemistry laboratory at Teledyne Isotopes in Westwood, NJ. Prior to this I graduated from Yale with a B.E. degree in Chemical Engineering, served four years in the Navy, received a Ph.D. degree in oceanography from Oregon State University, and performed two years of research for the Navy through the Defense Advanced Research Projects Agency.

Philip A. Johnson - *Introduction to Internet Protocols* and
Introduction to Business Data Communications
with Broadband and Wireless

I have written three books since graduating from Yale.

The first book, *Introduction to Business Data Communications with Broadband and Wireless* (2002), was written because I had the responsibility of teaching an MBA course in telecommunications in the Business School at William & Mary, and could not find a textbook that dealt with the real world.

The second book, *Introduction to Operating Systems* (2004), was written when I was teaching at Hampton University.

The third book, *Introduction to Internet Protocols* (2010), grew out of my experience serving on various national and international bodies concerned with specifying maintenance and operational standards for the Internet. I wanted to capture that experience in a brief book that would assist others who might become involved in the standards process.

Book description: This book discusses the architecture, protocols and features of TCP/IP and OSI. Of note is the discussion of protocol layering, hiding of information and the client-server principles underlying the various protocols, as well as a selection of various features of TCP/IP.

William F. Kay – *California Public Sector Labor Relations*

LOOK INSIDE!

This comprehensive treatise, updated each year, provides expert analysis of the labor relations statutes and case law covering California public sector labor relations. It is used by courts and by labor relations practitioners covering employees of over 4,000 state and local government units.

The treatise grew out of my discussion in 1986 with the General Counsel of the California Teachers Association, in which we both decried the quality of the legal work being done by both management and union attorneys. We concluded that one of the reasons for this less than sterling performance was the lack of a comprehensive treatise.

From that initial discussion we outlined a strategy for a comprehensive treatise. In the process we engaged over 50 union and management practitioners from the Labor Relations Section of the State Bar. This was a two-year labor of love involving the two originators and several key individuals.

Book description: *California Public Sector Labor Relations* brings you the authoritative, comprehensive guidance you need to answer most any question related to public sector labor relations in California in one convenient resource.

This comprehensive treatise provides labor attorneys, public sector employee organizations, public sector human resource personnel, and state and local public agency managers with an expert analysis of the statutes, case law, regulations, procedure, and agency decisions -- including PERB -- governing public sector labor relations in California.

This single volume offers broad coverage of the employer-employee relationship at all levels: state and local government, public school, community college, and state university.

Lindsey Kiang - *Huynh Phuong Dong: Visions of War and Peace*

The Vietnam War affected everyone in our Class, in one way or another. I myself did not participate in the War, but I went to Vietnam many years later. My numerous visits and interactions with the Vietnamese people made the history of the war come alive for me. This book, *Huynh Phuong Dong: Visions of War and Peace*, is a portrait of one of Vietnam's most beloved artists, whom I met during my earliest visits. An artist trained in the former French Fine Arts Academy in Hanoi, Mr. Dong's career as an artist was interrupted before it even started, as he spent nearly 30 years of his life in the army, fighting first the French and then the Americans. During those long years of war, he managed to record and document prodigiously the people and the events in the war-torn provinces surrounding the city of Saigon. At a time when it was unheard of for individuals to have cameras, Mr. Dong's paintings and sketches were a valuable part of the historical record of the Viet Cong's war in the South. I hope that the book will show not only that Fine Art knows no national boundaries, but also that the antagonists in that tragic war had much in common at the basic human level.

Book description: A richly illustrated introduction to the life and work of one of Vietnam's most esteemed artists. Produced in Vietnam under the auspices of the Indochina Arts Partnership and the Saigon Cultural Publishing House, this volume presents the work of Vietnamese artist Huynh Phuong Dong. He distinguished himself as a combat artist, creating sketches and drawings of scenes of battle, troops in action, and daily life in the guerilla bases, along with portraits of his comrades, both leaders and ordinary soldiers.

Many battle scenes are presented in nightmarish shades of red, reflecting the horror of combat. Dong's portraits are more intimate; he knew each subject and many of them did not survive the war. Dong himself was wounded in action in 1951 and again more seriously in 1969 during a B-52 air raid. He fought for twelve years and was separated from his wife for a decade. But he survived and in the process created a body of work that has come to be treasured in his country

J. Robert Kirkwood - *Essentials of Neuroimaging*

Essentials of Neuroimaging is a teaching book for senior radiology students preparing to take their American Board of Radiology examination. As an Associate Professor at Tufts University Medical School, teaching residents, I found that there was no good text for this purpose.

So, with great anxiety, I decided to do the book. Reviews were excellent. The New England Journal of Medicine, which normally doesn't review radiology books, began by saying, "Here is an excellent text." Writing the book, while practicing clinical work full time, was a two-year (X2) project that took me away from leisure family life.

Writing is awful; to have written is wonderful – for me. I am glad that I wrote the book, as it helps residents enormously, and the patients they will serve, and satisfied my wish to contribute to the medical profession in a global way. Thankfully, my family knew the importance, and supported the effort.

Book description: This is an introduction to neurological imaging, covering all elements essential to understanding how to make decisions about what modality to use for each neurological disease.

It is designed to serve as an introduction to the field, focusing on essentials for accuracy of diagnosis. It is heavily illustrated, including MRI. In most instances, the same patient is used to show how direct correlation between the various modalities.

Michael E. D. Koenig – *Knowledge Management*

This book is one of a series edited or co-edited by Mike Koenig on the subject of Knowledge Management (KM). KM can most easily be defined as equal parts of LIS (Library and Information Science), ICT (Information and Communication Technology), and HR (Human Relations) – not just organizing and communicating information more effectively, but changing the culture of the organization to make that happen.

Koenig lists more than 100 peer-reviewed publications on his vita. He has been the Dean of the Graduate School of Library and Information Science at Dominican University and Dean of the College of Information and Computer Science at Long Island University, where he is currently a Professor. He is a Past President of the International Society for Scientometrics and Infometrics.

Book description: *Knowledge Management* (KM) is an effort to increase useful knowledge in the organization. It is a natural outgrowth of late twentieth century movements to make organizational management and operations more effective, of higher quality, and more responsive to constituents in a rapidly changing global environment. This document traces the evolution of KM in organizations and the most influential research and literature in the field.

It also presents an overview of selected common and current practices in knowledge management, including the relationship between knowledge management and decision making, with the intention of making a case for KM as a series of processes and not necessarily a manipulation of things.

Rob Lacy - _Diagnosis: Cataract_

Diagnosis: Cataract

was written at a time when the technology for cataract surgery and intraocular lens implants was in its infancy. The book was written as a guide for patients with cataracts and considering cataract surgery.

Over a span of two years it sold about 6,600 copies. So many technological advancements have been developed over the past 30 years that the book is only of modest historical interest today and woefully outdated.

John Lahr – - _Notes on a Cowardly Lion_ - _Sinatra_ - _Coward the Playwright_ - _Tennessee Williams: Mad Pilgrimage of the Flesh_

Book descriptions: John Lahr's stunning and complex biography of his father, the legendary actor and comedian Bert Lahr. Part biography, part history of American show business, _Notes on a Cowardly Lion_ is John Lahr's masterwork: an all-encompassing biography of his father, the comedian and performer Bert Lahr. Best known as the Cowardly Lion in MGM's classic The Wizard of Oz, Lahr was a consummate artist whose career spanned burlesque, vaudeville, Broadway, and Hollywood.

While he could be equally raucous and polished in public, Lahr was painfully insecure and self-absorbed in private, keeping his family at arm's length as he quietly battled his inner demons. Told with an impressive objectivity and keen understanding of the construction—and destruction—of the performer, _Notes on a Cowardly Lion_ is more than one man's quest to understand his father. It is an extraordinary examination of a life on the stage.

John Lahr has produced a theater biography like no other. _Tennessee Williams: Mad Pilgrimage of the Flesh_ gives intimate access to the mind of one of the most brilliant playwrights of his century, whose plays reshaped the American theater and the nation's sense of itself. This deeply researched biography sheds light on Williams's warring family, his lobotomized sister, his guilt, his plays, his sexuality and numerous affairs, his misreported death, even the shenanigans surrounding his estate.

Here, in the sensational saga of Williams's rise and fall, Lahr captures not just the man's tempestuous public persona but also his backstage life, where Marlon Brando, Anna Magnani, Bette Davis, Maureen Stapleton, Diana Barrymore, Tallulah Bankhead, and Elia Kazan have scintillating walk-on parts. This is biography of the highest order: a book about the major American playwright of his time written by the major American drama critic of his time. 80 photographs

Jon H. Larson - *Self-Publish Your Own Book – a (simple) Guide*
Yale Class of 1963 Authors

Yale Class of 1963 - "Books by Class Authors"

This book seeks to motivate and enable readers to Self-Publish their own book(s).

Part I - "Self-Publish Your Own Book"
is an easy to follow step by step Guide that you can follow to self-publish your own book. It walks the reader through the process using the new generation of low cost and simple to use tools and services available online over the Internet to: 1) Complete your book into publishable form as a Hardcover or a Softcover book, and in Digital form as an eBook, 2) Introduce it into the distribution channels that will generate you sales revenue, and recognition and celebrity, at minimum upfront investment cost.
.

Part II - Yale Class of 1963 Authors
presents a collection of more than 100 books published by 81 Yale Class of 1963 authors, spanning an almost inconceivable variety of subject matters -- literary, artistic, musical, medical, legal, religious, scientific, historical, mathematical, political, autobiographical, and many more. It is a striking display of the many directions in which Yale 1963 classmates have taken their talents since graduation over a half century ago

Part III - Collective Wisdom of the Published Authors
Some of these books were self-produced using the new tools available today. Intimate Tips and Advice from the experienced Yale Class of 1963 published authors are shared with the reader.

Almost all of these books can be purchased online in hardcover, paperback, and electronic download form. This collection was assembled originally by Layton McCartney with the urging and support of 50th Reunion chairman Guy Struve for presentation at Sterling Memorial Library associated with the 50th Reunion of the Class of 1963.

Frank S. Letcher - *Mihail Chemiakin: Metaphysical Head:*
Deformation and Metamorphosis

Mihail Chemiakin: Metaphysical Head: Deformation and
Metamorphosis

was published by me in 1994 together with FERzT Books as a result of
my friendship with Chemiakin whom I consider to be the greatest
living Russian artist.

I have nurtured that deep interest in Russian language and culture
which was instilled in me by Yale. I asked Misha to prepare a lecture
on the subject of the human head for the Russian Neurosurgical
Society in St. Petersburg.

This book is the substance of that lecture: an explication of his artistic
theory of metaphysical synthetism as applied to the evolution of
images of the human head. In 2001, James H. Billington added this
book to the Library of Congress.

Michael Lieberman - *Bonfire of the Verities*

Although a research physician, I have had a second focus as a poet (and more recently as a novelist). Poetry has been my way of investigating those aspects of life not subject to empirical observation and demonstration, a way to process how one feels about the world rather than what one thinks about it. I have dealt with many subjects in my poems.

A book coming out this year *Bonfire of the Verities* treats the issues of faith, doubt, and those truths and beliefs we must discard as we age. Remnant is my attempt to process the Holocaust. There is nothing more to say other than the poems must speak for themselves. Far-From-Equilibrium Conditions takes as its premise the idea that like physical and political events (earthquakes, the market crash of 1929, and so on) authentic poetic experiences/revelations are outside the usual and put one in an emotional state of disequilibrium.

Book description: Res ipsa loquitor—the thing speaks for itself—as the lawyers say. But does it? Not in Michael Lieberman's new book of poems, *Bonfire of the Verities*. What speaks here is doubt and the commitment to cast aside the apparent truths we all accumulate. Those verities are what are tossed onto Lieberman's bonfire.

Thomas Lovejoy - *Climate Change and Biodiversity*

This is my second book on the interaction between climate change and the natural world (species and ecosystems). The first also published by Yale was 1992 when the best one could do was look at past (geological time) change and try and project forward. By the time this one was published in 2005 some early impacts were evident. So much has transpired since then that Lee Hannah and I are just starting a completely new book on the subject. Included in it will be the "good news" that proactive ecosystem restoration at scale (e.g. reforestation) could take back some of the atmospheric CO_2 burden and avoid maybe half a degree of climate change.

Book description: *"Climate Change and Biodiversity* provides the up-to-the-minute overview of this complex global interaction. It is a book of monumental importance to present to future generations and is a keystone work for science, policy and public understanding alike. Anyone concerned about the future of our planet and humanity needs this book." -Bruce Babbitt, former U.S. Secretary of the Interior.

"A well-written treatise on the past, present, and future effects of climate change on plant and animal biodiversity... It is destined to become a classic." -Choice. "This book makes a timely contribution in an important area. It is the only up-to-date, comprehensive, single book that covers the field of biodiversity in the context of climate change." -Brian Walker, CSIRO Sustainable Ecosystems, Canberra. "This book will be a milestone in the emerging discipline of climate change biology. No issue is more important for the global environment; the impressive line-up of experts here gives it definitive coverage." -Edward O. Wilson, Harvard University.

Barry Lydgate - *French in Action:*
**   *A Beginning Course in Language and Culture***

Barry Lydgate teaches at Wellesley College.

French in Action:

A Beginning Course in Language and Culture,

co-authored with Pierre J. Capretz and others, was first published in 1987, with subsequent editions in 1994 and 2013.

It is a wide-ranging introduction to French language, history, and culture.

Stephen R. MacKinnon - *Agnes Smedley:*
** *The Life and Times of an American Radical***

Agnes Smedley: The Life and Times of an American Radical (1988), written with my wife Janice Rachie MacKinnon, cemented the authors' marriage through a joint quest to understand the life story of one of America's more remarkable international journalists and feminists.

Smedley spent more than a decade after 1929 reporting on the Chinese revolution, and died suddenly in 1950 while under investigation by the FBI and Joe McCarthy for treason.

Book description: Country school teacher, birth control pioneer, socialist journalist, freedom fighter, writer--Agnes Smedley (1892-1950) was on the battlefront of American politics, the Indian struggle for independence, and the Chinese Communist revolution.

In this coherent, intelligible, and engaging book, the MacKinnons offer us a superb portrayal of one of the most significant female political figures in recent American history.

A more recent book ; Wuhan, 1938: War, Refugees, and the Making of Modern China (2008) focuses on the siege of Wuhan, which was the turning point militarily and politically in the Great War of 1937-1945 between Japan and China. In addition to the military history, the book describes the societal changes associated with the massive flight of refugees through Wuhan and the reshaping of culture and intellectual life in wartime China. I am pleased to say that the book in translation has reached a large audience in China.

Laton McCartney - _The Teapot Dome Scandal_
- Friends in High Places

In the interest of full disclosure, I should mention that my family benefited from some of the ill-gotten gains associated with the Teapot Dome affair. In 1935, my father, Frederick Laton McCartney, then going into his senior year at Yale, spent the summer in Europe. By the time he got to Paris in late August, my father was flat broke. Desperate, he called the only person he knew in the city, Harry M. Blackmer, and asked for a loan, explaining that he was Fred McCartney's son.

After satisfying himself that my father was telling the truth, Blackmer asked him to come right over to his apartment. There, my father enjoyed a lavish dinner with the old rogue and his Norwegian ingénue. Blackmer pumped him for news from home, and later presented him with $150 – a sizable sum in 1935 and more than enough to sustain my father until his ship departed a few days later.

Book description: _Friends in High Places_. The title reflects the author's characterization of the 80-year-old Bechtel Group, America's largest private company, which has incalculable resources and influences not only on U.S. foreign policy but on world events as well. Starting with its founder, entrepreneur Warren Bechtel, who built roads, railroads and other major projects like the Boulder Dam (constructed in alliance with Henry J. Kaiser), this engrossing account by freelance journalist McCartney traces the growth of the engineering firm's international operations under the leadership of the son and grandson during WW II and after, when the company won contracts for ships, planes, the Alaska Pipeline and nuclear plants.

The group's executives, McCartney contends, have filled or still occupy key posts in the White House, State Department, Pentagon and CIA, or have become CEOs of companies ready to further or protect Bechtel interests. The author also provides behind-the-scenes insights as to how the group covers up, if needed, questionable enterprises and conflicts of interest.

Thomas H. McGlashan –
A Developmental Model of Borderline Personality Disorder

Psychosis, also known as schizophrenia, is a serious mental disorder that develops in men and women most frequently between 15 and 30 years of age. The most well-known symptoms are hallucinations and delusions; the less well-known are incapacities in working and relating to others.

The disorder, once developed, must be treated indefinitely because it is irreversible once it has become full-blown. However, the signs and symptoms of psychosis initially develop over a period of months or years in late adolescence and early adulthood, and if it can be identified in this state of "psychosis-risk", treatment can prevent some, if not all, of the life-long damage that comes with the full-blown disorder. This book is a descriptive/diagnostic manual that provides clinicians with the knowledge and the means for identifying persons in this stage of psychosis-risk.

Book description: Patients with borderline personality disorder (BPD) are among the most challenging patients for clinicians to treat. Their behaviors and emotions can shift abruptly. As a result, these patients can seem like therapeutic moving targets, and improvement can be vexingly slow. *A Developmental Model of Borderline Personality Disorder* is a landmark work on this difficult condition.

*This book In*troduces the reader to a multidimensional and integrated etiologic model of BPD: Informs treatment -Helps clinicians develop the understanding and empathy needed to deal with difficult patient behaviors - Gives strategies for designing psychotherapy in tandem with psychosocial services to help patients with BPD improve or sustain functioning in the community. *A Developmental Model of Borderline Personality Disorder* combines rich clinical case descriptions with an integrated theoretical model that captures the complexities of BPD. This book is a first-rate clinical resource that reads like a novel, illuminating the disorder to help interpret its causes and course. It will inspire and encourage clinicians, along with patients and their family members, to strive for success in treating this difficult disease.

Williamson Murray – *- A War To Be Won*
                         - The Making of Strategy   *- Military Effectiveness*

These books represent three of a number of works that I have authored by myself, co-authored, or edited. They represent the fruit of my Yale education (B.A. 1963; Ph.D. 1975) and hard work since then. I have aimed my literary efforts at three distinct audiences: those in the general public interested in history, scholars, and officers in the armed forces of the United States as well as those who craft strategy to address the problems raised by a complex and dangerous world.

Book description: In the course of the twentieth century, no war looms as profoundly transformative or as destructive as World War II. Its global scope and human toll reveal the true face of modern, industrialized warfare. Now, for the first time, we have a comprehensive, single-volume account of how and why this global conflict evolved as it did. *A War To Be Won* is a unique and powerful operational history of the Second World War that tells the full story of battle on land, on sea, and in the air.

Williamson Murray and Allan R. Millett analyze the operations and tactics that defined the conduct of the war in both the European and Pacific Theaters. We see how strategies were crafted and revised, and how the multitudes of combat troops struggled to discharge their orders.

A War To Be Won is the culmination of decades of research by two of America's premier military historians. It avoids a celebratory view of the war but preserves a profound respect for the problems the Allies faced and overcame as well as a realistic assessment of the Axis accomplishments and failures. It is the essential military history of World War II--from the Sino-Japanese War in 1937 to the surrender of Japan in 1945--for students, scholars, and general readers alike.

William Nordhaus – *The Climate Casino:*
Risk, Uncertainty, and Economics for a Warming World

Having written many mathematically inclined and largely unreadable books and articles on macroeconomics and the environment, I decided to try a popular book on global warming. Much encouraged and inspired by classmate Tom Lovejoy, I planned to do it in three months but it took three years. Yale Press advised me to remove all equations from the text, although they would be allowed in endnotes.

Above all, I am stunned by the quantity and quality of books that have come from our class and are collected in this compendium. Keep writing.

Book description: Climate change is profoundly altering our world in ways that pose major risks to human societies and natural systems. We have entered the Climate Casino and are rolling the global-warming dice, warns economist William Nordhaus. But there is still time to turn around and walk back out of the casino, and in this essential book the author explains how.

Bringing together all the important issues surrounding the climate debate, Nordhaus describes the science, economics, and politics involved—and the steps necessary to reduce the perils of global warming. Using language accessible to any concerned citizen and taking care to present different points of view fairly, he discusses the problem from start to finish: from the beginning, where warming originates in our personal energy use, to the end, where societies employ regulations or taxes or subsidies to slow the emissions of gases responsible for climate change. Nordhaus is arguably the world's leading thinker on the economics of global warming. A Yale professor and president of the American Economic Association, he brings unassailable credibility to the central message of his new book: Climate change is an urgent economic issue with impacts that bear spiraling costs.

Robie Marcus Hooker "Mark" Palmer
– *Breaking The Real Axis of Evil:*
How to Oust the World's Last Dictators by 2025

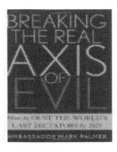

Mark Palmer had three careers after leaving Yale. First, he spent 26 years as a Foreign Service officer, co-writing President Reagan's 1982 Westminster speech (which led to the National Endowment for Democracy) and helping to accelerate the fall of Communism in Eastern Europe as United States Ambassador to Hungary.

Second, after the fall of the Berlin Wall, Mark founded an investment company to bring capitalism to the former Communist countries of Eastern Europe, including the first independent national commercial television stations in six post-communist countries. Third, Mark worked untiringly to advance the spread of democracy around the world, writing *The Real Axis of Evil: How to Oust the World's Last Dictators by 2025* and two manuals for diplomats and military officers on how they can support those struggling for freedom around the world.

Book description: In *Breaking the Real Axis of Evil*, ambassador Mark Palmer has the gumption to argue what diplomats and political leaders dare not speak: that global peace will not be achieved until democracies replace the world's remaining dictatorships. We know that these dictators are at the root of terrorism and war.

Under their stony gaze, millions have gone to their deaths, a great tidal wave of refugees has swept across the planet, and nations have been driven into poverty, famine, and despair. Drawing on over 25 years of extensive diplomatic experience, Ambassador Palmer asks us to embrace a bold vision of a world made safe by democracy. This is the story of the last 46 dictators, the strategy and tactics to oust them, and the need to empower the people of every nation to control their own destinies.

Gordon Clark Ramsey - *Agatha Christie: Mistress of Mystery*

Gordon Ramsey's *Agatha Christie: Mistress of Mystery* (1967) was the first biography of Dame Agatha Christie, and Gordon was the only one of Christie's biographers to have known Dame Agatha personally.

Gordon's love of literary mysteries was recognized in 2007, when Yale's Sherlock Holmes Society made him an honorary member in appreciation of a lecture he gave there.

Gordon was Assistant Executive Director of the Association of Yale Alumni during its formative years. He taught at the Worcester Academy and the University of Hartford. Gordon was an exceptional classical keyboard musician, and played the organ for the Class of 1963's first Memorial Service at the 40th Reunion

Anthony L. H. Rhinelander –
Prince Michael Vorontsov: Viceroy to the Tsar

As an undergraduate at Yale I studied the Russian language and majored in Russian Area Studies. Inspired by Firuz Kazemzadeh, one of my favorite professors, I decided to study the country of Georgia and its relationship to Russia. I completed my Ph.D. at Columbia University, where I studied the Georgian language.

I taught Russian History for 35 years at St Thomas University in Canada, designing among others a course in the history of Russian imperialism from the time of Ivan the Terrible to the formation of the Soviet Union. My research interests included studying the biographies of Russian imperial officials who organized the incorporation and administration of Georgia and the other Caucasian territories. One of the most interesting of those officials was a Russian aristocrat named Michael Vorontsov (1782-1886). My biography of him, entitled *Prince Michael Vorontsov: Viceroy to the Tsar*, was published by McGill-Queens University Press in 1990.

Book description: In *Prince Michael Vorontsov*, Anthony Rhinelander describes Vorontsov's pragmatic approach within a bureaucracy of legendary inefficiency and corruption. In New Russia Vorontsov dealt with problems such as famine and disease and helped to keep serfdom and religious persecution out of his territory. In Caucasia he made the local administration more effective by appointing Caucasian officials who were far more sensitive to the area's particular problems than were their Russian predecessors.

In fact, Vorontsov's Caucasian experience has relevance today it was recently suggested that present-day Soviet officials might have avoided some difficulty when dealing with Afghan rebels had they employed Vorontsov's tactics in handling armed guerillas. Rhinelander, whose extensive research included archival material available only in the Soviet Union, has written the first serious work on Vorontsov in English. Prince Michael Vorontsov will engage the interest and imagination of the general public and the historian.

William Pennell Rock - *Performing Inside Out*

ORIGINS is the organization I created to produce works of performing art based on ancient principles of sacred performance and contemporary methods of Jungian based psychodrama. The creative process combines psychotherapy, performance art, and mysticism. I have produced *ORIGINS* events throughout the U.S. and Europe as well as in Bali for many years, with great satisfaction and considerable success. *Performing Inside Out* describes the four stages of the *ORIGINS* process: CHAOS, DREAM, MYTH, and RITUAL.

It is about Theater.
It is about passion.
It is about myth.
It is about making authentic ritual drama.
It is about the process of individuation.
It is about dream.
It is about the entertainment of the future.
It is about good and evil.
It is about transformation.
It is about performing.
It is about the Spirit of Nature
It is about masks.
It is about Apollo and Dionysus.
It is about existence.
It is about our Time.
It is about Monsters.
It is about Being.
It is about survival.
It is about Nothing.
It is about the One.

John S. Rohsenow –

- A *Chinese-English Dictionary of Enigmatic Folk Similes*
- *ABC Dictionary of Chinese Proverbs (Yanyu)*
- *Modern Chinese Characters*

These books are some of the product of my forty years academic career of research and teaching linguistics and Chinese, primarily at the University of Illinois at Chicago, and in China and Taiwan. My *A Chinese-English Dictionary of Enigmatic Folk Similes* (Xiehouyu) [University of Arizona Press, 1991] is a collection of a little studied but extremely widespread popular expressions commonly used in spoken Chinese by which something is described metaphorically, but the resolution of the simile (often humorous) is left unsaid, thus leaving non-native speakers of Chinese (like me) in the dark as to the true meaning intended. This work received a Charles Tuttle Award for publications on Asian languages in 1992.

My *ABC Dictionary of Chinese Proverbs* (Yanyu) [University of Hawaii Press, 2001] is a similar collection/translation of 4000 commonly used Chinese Proverbs, both spoken and written in literature. It was reprinted in 2003, and also reprinted in China by the Hanyu Da Cidian Press, Shanghai,2002.

Modern Chinese Characters [Beijing: Sinolingua Press, 1994] is a reference textbook for students of Chinese interested in learning more about the history and structure of Chinese characters, especially as they are now used in mainland China. Chinese characters, with their unfamiliar rectangular outlines and complex structures, often appear to foreign learners to be an insuperable stumbling block. In fact, however, as long as the basic rules are grasped and right methods employed, it is not too hard to get started and it is also quite possible to gain a firm mastery of the written language. This book introduces in a lively and accessible way the origins, evolution, and composition of Chinese characters, their shapes, total numbers, pronunciation, meanings, and correct formations, as well as their dictionary ordering and consultation. The book aims to serve as a key to the fascinating realm of Chinese characters.

David Rudenstine - *The Day the Presses Stopped*

When the Nixon administration commenced a law suit against The New York Times (and later The Washington Post) seeking to enjoin the newspapers from publishing excerpts from what became popularly known as the Pentagon Papers, a Pentagon-sponsored history of U.S. involvement in Vietnam from World War II to 1968, the administration's legal action was widely characterized as a political vendetta.

That was certainly the position taken by the newspapers which dismissed as legal poppycock claims that disclosures from the "Top-Secret-Sensitive" 7000 page history threatened national security. Relying on court documents sealed during the litigation and interviews with most of the individuals central to the case, *The Day the Presses Stopped* argues that the newspapers' seminal victory in the Supreme Court was undoubtedly the right outcome, but that plausible national security considerations beset the lawsuit and that appreciating those considerations is essential to understanding the historic meaning of the Supreme Court's landmark ruling.

Book description: This bold account provides an original perspective on one of the most significant legal struggles in American history: the Nixon administration's efforts to prohibit the New York Times and the Washington Post from publishing the 7,000-page, top-secret Pentagon Papers, which traced U.S. involvement in Vietnam.

In his gripping account of this highly charged case, Rudenstine examines new evidence, raises difficult questions, and challenges conventional views of a historic moment.

John R. Sack - *The Franciscan Conspiracy*

The Franciscan Conspiracy is a spinoff of a young adult book I published in 1985, *The Wolf in Winter*. The earlier work described Francis of Assisi's youthful years. Research for that tale led me into this adult novel, a medieval history mystery that looks into several puzzles surrounding the life and death of Francis. Why was his body snatched during his funeral procession at the instigation of the Franciscan Order and hidden where it lay undiscovered for 600 years? Why did the Order demand that his early biographies be destroyed? And what lay behind the greatest mystery in his life, the stigmata impressed in his body two years before his death?

Published in 2005, *The Franciscan Conspiracy* has since been translated into 16 languages and was a top-10 bestseller in Germany, France and Holland, and for ten consecutive months in Brazil. I published a companion novel, *Angel's Passage*, in 2012. Other fiction includes *Love on a Rusty Spur* and *Trappist Tales*, a collection of short stories. Nonfiction work includes *Yearning for the Father*, published in 2006, and *Mystic Mountain*, published in 2013. Both describe the spiritual/mystical journey.

Book description: *The Franciscan Conspiracy*, a history mystery set in medieval Italy, has been published in 16 languages and has been a top-10 bestseller in Brazil and throughout Europe. On his death, Fra Leo, the closest companion of Francis of Assisi during the saint's life, leaves a cryptic message for a younger friar. He launches the young hermit Fra Conrad into a labyrinth whose every passage confronts his deepest fears—there to make sense of the bizarre and puzzling events that followed Francis' death in 1226.

The novel is set against the chaotic backdrop of 13th-century Italy, an era when the extreme poverty of religious zealots clashed with the burgeoning prosperity of merchants, the monastic orders and high-ranking Church officials. This chaos also divided the Franciscan Order after Francis' death.

Brian Salzberg – *Optical Methods in Cell Physiology*

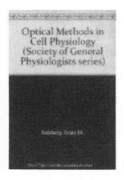

I edited this book, together with Professor Paul De Weer, more than a quarter of a century ago. It was the first book that included chapters on image enhancement, optical (molecular) probes of membrane voltage and intracellular calcium concentration, photo-activation, and photo-bleaching, in many cases before full reports were published by the contributors as papers.

All of these areas have since become "cottage industries" in Neuroscience, Physiology, and Biology generally, and the then-young authors went on to become leaders in their respective fields. The techniques that were described in this book have been used, in the ensuing 27 years, in many thousands of publications.

Book description: A book for physiologists, biologists and biochemists studying cell physiology. Included are major optical techniques and bases for designing experiments and choosing appropriate instrumentation, along with discussions on methods and results of optical techniques applied to research through image enhancement, probes for membrane potential, intracellular indicators for Ca and pH, and photo-bleaching and photo-activation techniques. Also included are schematic drawings and numerous references.

Stanton Samenow - _Inside the Criminal Mind_

Inside the Criminal Mind provides a view of the thinking processes of individuals who have made crime a way of life. It explains why I abandoned a "conventional wisdom" that regards criminal behavior as a product of one's environment or of a mental illness.

The book has stirred controversy within the field of criminal psychology and criminology. It has become a textbook for many professionals in law enforcement and corrections. The Myth of the Out of Character Crime takes sharp issue with the view that people commit crimes because life becomes too much for them and they "snap" and act out of character.

I discuss specific cases, including that of the youthful Washington, D.C. sniper, Lee Boyd Malvo, and take issue with the view that the people described were basically good guys who turned bad. _Before It's Too Late_ addresses the thorny issue of early identification and prevention of antisocial/criminal conduct. This book, first published in 1989 and revised in 1999, has brought relief to many parents who experience far too much guilt for the conduct of their offspring.

Book description: Long-held myths defining the sources of and cures for crime are shattered in this ground-breaking book--and a chilling profile of today's criminal emerges.

William F. Sanford, Jr. - *The American Business Community and the European Recovery Program, 1947-1952*

The American Business Community and the European Recovery Program, 1947-1952 began as a Ph.D. dissertation subsequently published by Garland as part of a 24 book series on U.S. foreign economic policy. My own interest were the activities and actions of American businessmen regarding European recovery after World War II, the broad goal of Marshall Plan assistance. I discovered that although there was some opposition in Congress and among certain industries to certain aspects of the aid program, businessmen generally supported it. They believed that the long-term economic interests of both their industries and the nation would best be served by prompt and effective European recovery despite short-term sacrifices. This was certainly the case among the businessmen who administered the aid program, Paul Hoffman, and others who were former industry executives. It was also true of many smaller businessmen. Some were even willing to divulge closely held production methods during European technical visits as long as their foreign counterparts agreed to share their own manufacturing techniques in return.

My work on the manuscript extended beyond graduate school to my early years in the State Department Historian's Office and depended heavily on State and AID materials, most of which were scheduled to be transferred to the National Archives. Unfortunately not all my source material made it that far. Some of the most revealing documents I found were the reports and correspondence of European industrial teams visiting American factories to learn more about U.S. production methods. Unfortunately these papers were part of a large bloc of technical assistance records that National Archives appraisers concluded had little historical value. Before these records were destroyed, I received permission to remove the 3 cubic feet of documents that I used for my manuscript. These files finally found a permanent home and are currently preserved as the "ECA technical Assistance Papers, 1948-1952 in the Smithsonian Archives at the National Museum of American History in Washington, D.C.

Murray Sargent III - _Laser Physics_

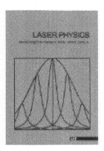

Laser Physics describes the semi-classical and fully quantal theories of the laser as understood in the 1970's. As the junior author, I did most of the work, but my coauthors added significantly to the content and success of the book. The book doesn't describe semiconductor lasers, which are probably the most important. Later on when semiconductor lasers were better understood, I coauthored a book on them.

Laser Physics is a classic in its field and remains in print as a paperback. _Interfacing Microcomputers to the Real World_ is my first book about microcomputers. It grew out of a couple of efforts, namely computerizing my home and creating a technical word processor. My Ph.D. advisor, Willis Lamb, Jr., was fond of saying that a real physicist should do both theory and experiment.

So I figured computerizing my home would be a kind of experiment! It was many years before the infrastructure for computerizing homes efficiently arrived, but our little book helped things along. It was typeset using my technical word processor, PS. It prefaces chapters with deep observations, such as, "At first it seems like magic; it's really just plain logic!"

Book description: This book treats the interaction of radiation with matter, particular attention being paid to the laser. Knowledge is assumed of the usual half-year introduction of quantum mechanics found in undergraduate physics curricula. The material can be covered in two semesters, or, alternatively, the first part (Chaps 1-13) can be used as a one-semester course in which quantum mechanical aspects of the electromagnetic field are ignored.

Each chapter is accompanied by problems that illustrate the text and give useful (occasionally new) results. Existing laser media are intrinsically quantum mechanical and are most easily studied with the quantum theory. Understanding the laser along these lines enlivens one's understanding of quantum mechanics itself. In fact, the material constitutes a viable, applied alternative for the usual second and third semesters of quantum mechanics.

Fredric T. Schneider - *The Art of Japanese Cloisonné Enamel:*
History, Techniques and Artists, 1600 to the Present

In 1992, still deep in my Wall Street career, I was moved by exhibitions at The Metropolitan Museum of Art and Japan Society to begin a serious collection of Japanese art that could ultimately be donated to one or more museums. I was initially uncertain in which particular specialty to focus my collection.

In addition to the beauty and virtuosity of the art, my other primary criterion was that it be a field to which I might ultimately make a substantial scholarly contribution because of the relative absence of previous scholarly attention.

The Art of Japanese Cloisonné Enamel: History, Techniques and Masters, 1600 to the Present, the product of over 17 years of collecting and research and now considered the definitive work in its field, is part of my endeavor to honor that criterion. My life has been greatly enriched by my decision to reengage in extended scholarly pursuit and by my choice of cloisonné enamel.

Book description: An art form renowned for its beauty and technical wizardry, Japanese cloisonné enamel is receiving increased attention from collectors, museum curators and art historians. This book provides a detailed history of Japanese cloisonné enamel and the development of its many technical varieties. Part One presents the 400-year history and socio-political-economic context of Japanese enamels from their beginnings around 1600 to the present, covering extensively in particular the crucial decades of the late 19th and early 20th centuries. Part Two is organized by individual technique and categorizes and discusses the many variations of cloisonné enamel developed in Japan.

Integrated into both parts are biographies of dozens of cloisonné masters along with discussions of the technical and scientific underpinnings of the craft. The work is complemented by an extensive glossary, several appendices, and a guide to identifying 290 artist marks and signatures.

Jerry Selness – *Primitive Benchmark:*
A Short Treatise on a General Theory of Sailing

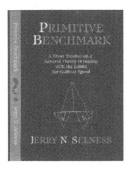

This book chronicles a discovery I made that led to a powerful and beautiful general theory for all sailboats and sailing craft.

I am a pilot and have a Master's degree from the University of California at Berkeley in Naval Architecture.

The book is in libraries in more than 20 countries at last count. It is on the reserve shelf in some libraries.

I am a thinker, always thinking, asking questions, grateful for my Yale beginnings.

Edward R. Shapiro - *Lost in Familiar Places*

I wrote *Lost in Familiar Places* with the former Dean of Westminster Abbey, Wesley Carr. Our collaboration was an unusual one, bringing together an American Jewish psychoanalyst and an English Anglican priest. We met as staff members in a Tavistock Group Relations conference, an experiential exploration of the organizational and social dynamics around the exercise of leadership and authority.

I came to our shared thinking from psychoanalysis and the study of individuals and families; Wesley came from a deep immersion in the relationship between institutions and society. We brought these perspectives together in this book. The book is still in print after 22 years. We are all still trying to discover how to find a voice as individuals in such a turbulent society.

Book description: We live in a world of accelerating change marked by the decline of traditional forms of family, community, and professional life. Both within families and in workplaces individuals feel increasingly lost, unsure of the roles required of them. In this book a psychoanalyst and an Anglican priest, using a combination of psychoanalysis and social systems theory, offer tools that allow people to create meaningful connections with one another and with the institutions within which they work and live.

The authors begin by discussing how life in a family prefigures and prepares the individual to participate in groups, offering detailed case studies of families in therapy as illustrations. They then turn to organizations, describing how their consultations with an academic conference, a mental hospital, a law firm, and a church parish helped members of these institutions to relate to one another by becoming aware of wider contexts for their experiences. According to Shapiro and Carr, when individuals can negotiate a shared interpretation of the experience and of the purposes for which the group exists, they can further their own development and that of their organizations. The authors suggest how this can be accomplished. They conclude with some broad speculations about the continuing importance of institutions for connecting the individual and society.

Harvey B. Simon - *Staying Well*

After only a few years in medical practice, I realized that health is too important to be left to doctors. Good health depends on collaboration between patients and physicians; to get the best results, doctors must be sure their patients understand the simple rules of the road that can enhance health, improve the quality of life, and reduce the chances of falling ill.

I wrote *Staying Well* to help readers understand how their bodies work, how to stay healthy, and how to work with their doctors to choose the best treatments when problems develop. As the third of six books, *Staying Well* marked the mid-point in my consumer health writing career.

It was my longest and most difficult book, but the research that went into it set the stage for subsequent books and for the monthly newsletter, *Harvard Men's Health Watch*, that I wrote from 1996 to 2012. Most important, writing for the public made me a better clinician. After all, the root for "doctor" is "docere", to teach. Writing is teaching, and teaching is learning.

Book description: Explains how readers can take health into their own hands with the Ten Commandments of Prevention and twenty-three chapters filled with the latest research and advice on how to lower the risk of acquiring the most deadly diseases. 15,000 first printing.

Tom Stempel - *FrameWork: A History of Screenwriting in the American Film* and *American Audiences on Movies and Moviegoing*

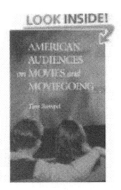

I have written six books about film, five of them about screenwriting. The first book on exhibit here, *FrameWork: A History of Screenwriting in the American Film*, is the first history of screenwriting in American film. It was described by screenwriter Philip Dunne as "the definitive work on the history of screenwriting." It has gone to three editions, and has been used as a textbook in university courses.

The second book, *American Audiences on Movies and Moviegoing*, is the black sheep among my books, since it is not about screenwriting.

It is a history of American film from 1948 to 2000 from the audiences' perspective: what did the audience (not the critics or historians) think about movies and the moviegoing experience. The comments from ordinary moviegoers appalled academic reviewers of the book, since "real people" do not think about movies and movie going the way academics think they should.

Book description: *Framework:* Stempel traces the development of the script and screenwriter in the Hollywood film. Beginning with the early film shorts, he shows the evolution of the brief story outline into the full-scale epic screenplay. With the rise of the studio system, he outlines the decline of the screenwriter in the overall hierarchy and the emergence of the screenwriter/producer or director.

Woven throughout are brief vignettes of producers, directors, stars, and, of course, screenwriters. Combining scholarship with movie lore, Stempel has produced an informative and readable work. Recommended for large film collections

Phillips Stevens, Jr. - *The Stone Images of Esie, Nigeri*
and
Anthropology of Religion: Critical Concepts in Religious Studies

 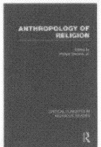

The Stone Images of Esie, Nigeria (1978) helped to bring world-wide attention to a collection of about 1000 soapstone sculptures of unknown age and purpose, most of great sculptural merit. For my work there, in 2012 I was conferred with an honorary chieftancy by the traditional ruler of the town.

My title is Chief Erewumi of Esie Kingdom; the name means, roughly, "The images and I get along well."

Anthropology of Religion: Critical Concepts in Religious Studies (2011) is the fruit of an invitation from the venerable British publishing house, Routledge, to edit a work in their series "*Critical Concepts in Religious Studies.*"

The result was the largest edited collection of writings in the field (80 items), which, along with the opportunity to express my own theories of religion in the 50-page Introduction, outweighed the burden of the long and heavy work load involved in editing the work.

Book description: Religious belief is a powerful motivator of human behaviour. Religious considerations permeate and influence all parts of a culture. Religious systems are universal, around the world and through all stages of human history and prehistory. The anthropological approach is the most comprehensive and the most useful to students of human belief and behaviour, because it examines religion as a cultural system that cannot fully be understood separated from the other systems with which it interacts.

This new four-volume collection from Routledge assembles exemplary scholarship in the field from its Victorian beginnings to the present, and represents all generally accepted categories of religious belief and ritual, plus some new ones. Topics covered include: 'Early Explorations'; 'Symbols'; 'Supernatural Beings'; 'Magical Power and Forces'; 'Human Agents of Supernatural Danger'; 'Myth'; 'Ritual'; 'Religious Practitioners'; 'Women and Gender'; 'Belief'; 'Ecology'; 'Mind and Body—Neurobiological Bases'; and 'Religion in Socio-Cultural Change'.

Samuel N. Stokes - *Saving America's Countryside:*
A Guide to Rural Conservation

Saving America's Countryside: A Guide to Rural Conservation, first published in 1989, was the culmination of my work for the National Trust for Historic Preservation. I established the Trust's Rural Program to focus national attention on the importance of protecting America's rural historic resources and their natural settings. The Washington Post described the book as "a collective voice raised for small towns, farms, and nature's wonders, and a conviction that hard-focused work can change the course of events for the better."

The Journal of the American Planning Association called it "the preeminent land-use-oriented reference work for rural communities." I met my wife Sally while doing research for the book at the University of Maryland, where she was in charge of the historic preservation library.

Book description: The second edition of *Saving America's Countryside*, published by Johns Hopkins University Press in 1997, is a guide to protecting a rural community's natural, historic, scenic, and agricultural resources. The coauthors--Samuel N. Stokes, A. Elizabeth Watson, and Shelley S. Mastran--describe how community leaders can organize a conservation effort, inventory resources, pass protective ordinances, establish land trusts, obtain outside assistance, and assure public support. The book includes numerous illustrations and 32 case studies that describe a variety of successful local conservation programs from across the country.

William D. Sudderth - *Discrete Gambling and Stochastic Games*

Discrete Gambling and Stochastic Games is a contribution to the pure mathematics of probability and game theory. It can be viewed as a sequel to the book *How to Gamble If You Must: Inequalities for Stochastic Processes*, written by my Ph.D. thesis adviser Lester Dubins and Leonard Savage.

Those authors quote Louis Bacheller, who said (in translation from the French): "[I]t is gambling that gave birth to the calculus of probability; it is to gambling that this calculus owes its first faltering utterances and its most recent developments; it is, therefore, gambling that we must strive to understand. But one should understand it in a philosophic sense, free from all vulgar ideas."

Book description: (from Springer-Verlag, a long-time prolific publisher of math and science). The theory of probability began in the seventeenth century with attempts to calculate the odds of winning in certain games of change. However, it was not until the middle of the twentieth century that mathematicians developed general techniques for maximizing the chances of beating a casino or winning against an intelligent opponent. These methods of finding optimal strategies are at the heart of the modern theory of stochastic control and stochastic games.

This monograph provides an introduction to the ideas of gambling theory and stochastic games. The first chapters introduce the ideas and notation of gambling theory. Chapters 3 and 4 consider "leavable" and "non-leavable" problems which form the core theory of this subject. Chapters 5, 6, and 7 cover stationary strategies, approximate gambling problems, and two-person zero-sum stochastic games respectively.

Throughout, the authors have included examples and there are problem sets at the end of each chapter.

Fritz Thiel - *Der Raum, wo nur als Geist du liebst*

Der Raum, wo nur als Geist du liebst (The Realm Where You Only Love as a Spirit) initially contains forty German poems by Friedrich Heinrich Thiel (1870-1929), my grandfather and a preacher and administrator in the German speaking synod of the Methodist Church. Originating in the early 1800s, the German Methodist church in the United States flourished until the First World War. Then anti-German sentiment, including public burnings of German books, undermined the further existence of German in the United States. His poems bear witness to his strong Christian beliefs.

My own poems then follow and number around 188. The first twenty-five in *Wort und Laut (Word and Sound)* are all comprised of two rhyming stanzas of four lines each. *Deutsche Sonette (German Sonnets)* contains 100 sonnets. Many utilize standard rhyme schemes common in Western literature. Because so many rhymes have become commonplace, I frequently use assonance instead of pure rhyme. The final collection, *Urbilder (Primeval Images),* displays diverse poetic forms and metrics.

My poems have always focused on human relationships and individual personalities. Timeless topics such as art, beauty, love, God, temporality, human tragedy, and death also emerge repeatedly. I rarely if ever address social and political issues.

Haag and Herchen in Frankfurt, Germany, published the book in 1996. I subsidized it. Prior to publication, a German editor well-versed in poetry studied the book carefully and, when necessary, engaged me in stimulating discussions on the poems. Since publication, perhaps 750 copies of the book have been sold. Composer Curt Cacioppo, Harvard Ph. D. and Ruth Marshall Magill professor of music at Haverford College, set seven of the poems to music. The resulting CD is entitled *Burning with the Muse* and contains the *Sieben Thiel Lieder (Seven Thiel Songs).* In 2005 I published two longer essays entitled *Meißen und Mahagoni: Amerika, wie es nicht jeder sieht (Meissen and Mahagony: America as not Seen by Everyone.)* In 2013 both of my books were reviewed and accepted into the German National Literature Archive at Marbach near Stuttgart.

Gordon Thorne - *__Area Collection__*

Area Collection was published in 1972, and took two years to assemble.

In 1970, 100 letters were sent through the mail, predominantly to artists, asking them to send me back 200 copies of an 8.5" x 11" "page" which I would assemble into 100 books. Each person would get two copies of the book in one binding.

It was not as easy 40 years ago to reproduce images. Some of the pages were hand altered, and some were perishable. As a result, there were less than 100 copies actually mailed, and thus there were several extra "bound" copies, of which this is one. The Yale New Haven Post Office did not consider *Area Collection* to be a book. I did. This is the first edition. There never was a second edition.

This book was published in the early 1970's, an era that was:
     -pre –personal computing,
     -pre Internet,
     -pre-digital cameras,
     -pre-digital processing, and
     -pre- low cost laser printing technology.

Producing a book required "cut and paste", manual processing, the U.S. Postal Service, and handling by many people. And it was laborious and expensive to alter and re-produce updated versions.

A.O. Dennis Willows – _Neurobiology and Behavior_

After Yale (Physics), I went to graduate school in neurobiology at University of Oregon, ostensibly to solve the problem of the brain. The decades following 1963 saw dramatic growth in interest and progress in nervous system studies worldwide.

My small part of this was to develop knowledge of the largest brain cells in the animal kingdom, found in mollusks, as useful models for study of how neural circuits are interconnected and produce coherent patterns of nerve impulses that generate recognizable patterns of behavior.

I published about 50 scientific papers, many with co-authors, and a few books on the topic, and this one is a sample. The excitement engendered by discoveries in neurophysiology continues even into the present with a major initiative in 2013, promoted by the U.S. President via federal research agencies.

Richard Worley - *Hypertension in Pregnancy*

After college, medical school, and residency in obstetrics and gynecology, I did a fellowship in reproductive endocrinology at the University of Texas in Dallas. My mentor and I conducted studies of placental hormone synthesis in which we quantitated the conversion of precursor to product hormones (in this case estradiol), as well as alterations in placental blood flow.

We found that placental blood flow is reduced in women with pre-eclampsia, the commonest form of hypertension in pregnancy. We also found that diuretic administration, widely used for pre-eclampsia at the time, further reduced placental blood flow, additionally imperiling the fetus.

We wrote *Hypertension in Pregnancy* to summarize then-current information about these disorders, to emphasize the adverse effect of both hypertension and diuretic treatment on placental blood flow, and to outline preferred modes of management, which remain current today.

Part III
Collective Wisdom of the Published Authors
Notes and comments from the Yale Class of 1963 Authors on getting published...

Collective Wisdom of the Authors

1) Agents and Publishers:

As an academic, all of my books have been published by university presses or the equivalent. In some cases, they have come looking for manuscripts; in others, I have approached them. In each case, the procedure is pretty much the same. The publisher asks for a brief statement of the book's objective, followed by a chapter by chapter summary. Most publishers will send that document to a couple of anonymous reviewers for advice on whether to go further.

Assuming the responses are positive, the publisher will then ask for the complete manuscript which will be sent out for a more complete evaluation by (possibly the same) anonymous reviewers. Their comments and your responses (e.g., changes you wish to make in the wake of the comments, or why you may disagree with some comments) then go to a meeting of the various editors at the publishing house at which a decision is made on whether to publish. Assuming that decision is positive, a contract is signed by both parties, and the editorial process begins. The publisher bears all publication costs except the cost of preparing an index, which is left to the author, or (more likely) a professional who the author hires. The publisher also sets the price.

All publishers promise significant marketing, but in my view generally do less than is promised. Certainly, the print advertising of academic books seems to have declined somewhat. But one change that was quite evident when my book on symphony economics appeared is the important role of blogs and bloggers. These now exist on all manner of topics and have both pluses and minuses, in my view. A virtue is that they get the word out much more rapidly than print media (and long before formal professional book reviews appear). Well-informed bloggers can do a lot to make the existence of a book known and influence its initial sales.

Of course, the important words are "well-informed." I have benefited from well-informed bloggers, who took the time to read the book carefully before commenting. But there is no protection from parties who may have an ax to grind or have not even read the book. For example, I discovered that Amazon reviewers may not even have read the book -- the first two reviews I received (both very low) were from people who stated that they would not read the book because they objected to the high price placed on it by the publisher. There are aspects of the blogosphere that are perhaps too democratic!   BF

2) Publishing for perfection, tenure, and for self:

From the beginning my books have been published by academic or commercial presses. Thus, with my own editing (which by the way is a pain in the rear because you never get all the errors -- nor do your editors) and the help of the editors at the various presses who have been very good (but they can be a pain in the rear as well because they always want to change things that you don't want changed).

I have been able to produce works that are largely free of errors. In addition, the presses have done virtually all of the work in terms of book design and cover design, although I still go back and forth with them over the picture on the cover. I now either send my stuff to Cambridge (with whom I have a very good relationship) or go through an agent who has done some pretty useful digging for me.

I got in the writing business because I wanted to get tenure (my primary aim in going to graduate school after my tour in Southeast Asia was to teach at the college level), and the more I did of it the better, I believe, I got. Some parts of it I love -- the trying to solve a puzzle (what makes an effective, adaptive, and innovative organization for example); other parts of it I hate: **any worthwhile writing demands rewriting, rewriting, and rewriting**. And God do I hate to rewrite (I'd almost rather have a tooth pulled). And worst of all is the problem of editing as the manuscript moves to page proofs. By that time I am so bored by the whole thing that I'd like to burn the galleys. But I plug along looking for the tiniest mistakes, because reviewers love to nail you for mistakes.

I have an outstanding grasp of English grammar (hammered into my head at an early age), but I am hopeless as a speller -- thank God for spell check. What I am willing to do is read any interesting manuscripts in the field of history, journalism or current affairs and give whoever sends it to me some feedback as to whether it is publishable (for a bottle of good single malt).

And if It's really good I can recommend my agent. WM

For Self: Just think of your manuscript as a rough diamond, that through countless cuts and polishes (edits), the blemishes are removed one by one and the eventual result is the beautiful flawless perfect diamond (your book) that emerges slowly from within.   JL

3) Marketing and Promotion:

I published through traditional channels, although it took about six years to come out because of health issues with the publisher. It wasn't until he sold the press that the new owner released the book. This was fortunate in a way. I finished it before _DaVinci Code_ came out, but it was published after that blockbuster bestseller, and everyone was looking for the "next" DaVinci. Apparently many foreign publishers thought my book was it, and it did in fact do quite well.

Since then I have self-published a number of books under my CyberScribe Publications imprint. Mostly I've used CreateSpace, and Kindle for the Amazon eBook. I've also used Smashwords to create other-than-Kindle platforms, although it can be quite awkward, especially if you're writing nonfiction and have a slew of footnotes.

The hardest part for me has been marketing and promotion. I've collected a list of marketing suggestions, but frankly keep so busy writing and blogging that I don't have time to market. Nor do I care much for that process.

Thank goodness I don't have to rely on royalties to survive, although that would probably be a motivator.   JS

---

4) Working with Editors:

Nunnally Johnson was the great American screenwriter of _The Grapes of Wrath _and many others. It was my doctoral dissertation at UCLA and the first biography of a screenwriter to focus on his contributions to his films. It was turned down by over thirty publishers, most of them twice. The project began when I did a long oral history interview with Nunnally at UCLA. We first tried to sell it as an interview book, but nobody was buying. One publisher said he would like to buy the research and hire a writer to write a biography. The agent I had at the time suggested I write the book, and the publisher replied, "Oh, no, we want to hire a PROFESSIONAL writer." I told the agent I was perfectly willing to turn pro, but he knew the publisher would not go for it. Later I had another agent who set me up with a meeting with a New York editor who was in Los Angeles shopping for writers.

The only thing the editor asked me was if the book would be funny. I told him that it would since Nunnally was one of the great wits in Hollywood, but that the heart of the book was Nunnally's artistic contributions to his films as a screenwriter. The editor got a look on his face that said, "*What planet are you from?*" I read Andrew Sarris [the film critic who promoted directors] in the Village Voice so I know that directors make it all up as they go along. Later I had a contract with the University Press of California, which indicated the manuscript would be read by two readers. If they agreed it should be published, it would be. If they disagreed, a third reader would give an opinion. When I finished the first draft, I sent it to my editor there saying I just wanted his notes and not to send it to readers.

A few months later I had not heard from him and wrote to him. He told me the first reader loved it and he was sure the second reader would to. Well, the second reader not only did not like it, but hated it in such virulent terms that the editor felt that even if a third reader liked it, the second reader's comments were such that the editorial board would not approve it. Later on I had another agent who ended up sending it to the list of publishers I gave her as places NOT to send it. Finally a friend suggested a publisher he had dealt with and they decided to publish it. None of the agents I have ever had have ever sold any of my work. Two of the agents I had on the first book did things that damaged the selling process, and one of them did it deliberately to help one of her other clients. It may or may not surprise you to learn that she went on to become a producer of movies, mostly bad ones that flopped. I've had to do it myself. SCREENWRITER was published to good reviews and is still quoted from in other books about film and screenwriter, as is FRAMEWORK.

As for helpful insights about the publishing business, the best I can offer is STAY AWAY FROM IT. The next best is this: If they (whoever "they" are) won't let you do THIS, do THAT. I supposed I followed that on my first book. You don't want to publish it, o.k., I'll find somebody else who will. While I was working on that book, I began to collect stories on successful books that were turned down by publishers. There are a lot of them.

The general rule is you get turned down by about 15 publishers before you find one. I must say that on my other books, I generally was only turned down by one or two, and in a couple of cases, I did books that the publisher asked me to do. On my last book in 2008, I was back up to ten rejections before I found a publisher. TS

5) On Reviews and Critics:

My favorite review was by Larry Summers, who wrote, *"There is more insight and good sense advice in this volume than in many libraries."*

My least favorite was one dripping in scorn by Dr. J in *Science* magazine, but I was relieved when someone emailed me and said that "J" was behaving like a jacka__ once again.

Another colleague praised it highly but was skeptical that – in the age of Twitter – people would read anything that required actually turning a page. He once said that the attention span of most Americans is shorter than one true sentence.

Above all, I am stunned by the quantity and quality of books that have come from our class and are collected in this compendium. Keep writing!   BN

---

6) Way back when:

My co-author and I were published by Appleton-Century by what I remember as a kind of mutual agreement. They asked us if we would consider producing a work on hypertension in pregnancy. We did so, and they accepted the manuscript.

Thirty-five years ago, as we all remember, circumstances were so different from those of today. The manuscript was dictated, transcribed, rewritten, and edited until "perfect" (couldn't stand to read it another time), and submitted.   RW

---

7) Editing: (for content and for grammar)

One of my Author colleagues retains two editors. One for content, and a second for grammer [sic].

It is painful to have the content editor expert slice and dice up your carefully constructed work.
  - Losing a word is painful.
  - Losing a paragraph is like losing a finger.
  - Losing an entire section is like having a surgeon remove a limb.   JL

8) For seniors wanting to publish for the first time:

There are at least four factors that might be preventing us from self-publishing that first book.

a) <u>Feeling dated</u> and that our contributions might not be worthy because our views and experience are out of date with the real world today and its more immediate priorities.

b) Shameless <u>self-promotion</u> is difficult for us.

c) Many of us are <u>computer/keyboarding challenged.</u>

d) We might not be as <u>mentally acute</u> as earlier in our careers.

8-a) Publishing Across Generations:

Our Yale 1963 class followed the greatest generation of our mothers and fathers, the WW II seniors that Tom Brokaw describes in his book *The Greatest Generation,* America's citizen heroes and heroines who came of age during the Great Depression and the Second World War and went on to build modern America. This greatest generation was united not only by a common purpose, but also by common values— duty, honor, economy, courage, service, love of family and country, and, above all, responsibility for oneself. They were self-effacing, team oriented, humble, loyal to the group, suppressed individualism and promoted group achievement. And they did it all without *"#hashtags".*

We are sandwiched in between **the Greatest Generation** and the **Boomers** who started arriving 5-10 years after us, with **the X generation** coming along behind them. Promoting themselves with "selfies" on their cell phones and sharing the most mundane moments of daily life with photos shared on FaceBook contrasts with our generation's typical views reflected in Betty White's on-TV comment on *Saturday Night Live* that *"FaceBook is a gigantic waste of time."*

Generation X encompasses the 44 to 50 million Americans born between the early 1960's and the early 1980's. This generation marks the period of birth decline after the baby boom and is significantly smaller than previous and succeeding generations.

Members of Generation X are largely in their 30's and early 40's. On the whole, they are more ethnically diverse and better educated than the Baby Boomers. Over 60% of Generation X attended college.

Below are a few common characteristics of Generation X taken from www.about.com.

Individualistic: Generation X came of age in an era of two-income families, rising divorce rates and a faltering economy. Women were joining the workforce in large numbers, spawning an age of "latch-key" children. As a result, Generation X is independent, resourceful and self-sufficient. In the workplace, Generation X values freedom and responsibility. Many in this generation display a casual disdain for authority and structured work hours. They dislike being micro-managed and embrace a hands-off management philosophy.

Technologically Adept: The Generation X mentality reflects a shift from a manufacturing economy to a service economy. The first generation to grow up with computers, technology is woven into their lives. As businesses integrate new technological tools, Generation X has learned and adapted. This generation is comfortable using PDAs, cell phones, e-mail, laptops, Blackberry's and other technology employed in the workplace.

Flexible: Many Gen Xers lived through tough economic times in the 1980s and saw their workaholic parents lose hard-earned positions. Thus, Generation X is less committed to one employer and more willing to change jobs to get ahead than previous generations. They adapt well to change and are tolerant of alternative lifestyles. Generation X is ambitious and eager to learn new skills but wants to accomplish things on their own terms.

Value Work/Life Balance: Unlike previous generations, members of Generation X work to live rather than live to work. They appreciate fun in the workplace and espouse a work hard/play hard mentality. Generation X managers often incorporate humor and games into work activities.

Your book needs to consider its **appeal to ALL of the generations who will be reading it,** while avoiding "preaching only to your own choir." JL

8-b) Shameless Self-promotion and Relevancy:

Self-promotion: Boomers and the X generation are able to self-promote more naturally. Our senior generation's more natural instincts are to perform but let others take the credit, including leaving promoting one's own book to others. But self-publishing by definition requires us to stand up and "shout out." To sell a book requires shameless self-promotion about our own capabilities and experiences that are documented in the Author's Bio section of our books.

To those of us in our '70's looking to self-publish our first book, we need to take lessons from the Boomers and X generations behind us. Step up and self-promote. A must best read on the subject is _How to Self-Promote (without being a jerk)_ by Bruce Kasanoff.

Relevancy: Incorporate the best aspects of the younger generations today. Don't judge yourself. Just put it out there and let the world judge you. Consider their interests as a larger audience who should want to purchase your book. Be relevant to their needs. And if you do not like certain criticism you hear, just consider the source, and tune into the majority positive folks giving you the good reviews rather than obsessing on the minority negative criticism.   JL

8-c) Being computer/keyboard challenged:

Most of us were introduced to personal computers and keyboarding in our later years when our brains were already mostly filled with other stuff including skills and important relationships connections and not as able to absorb the manual dexterity required by new skills including keyboarding and the often strange interfaces of computers.

If we were lucky we took a typewriting course in private high school. In college we paid others to type our handwritten papers at a fixed cost per word. And at work, we turned our handwritten notes over to the typing pool or later were able to transcribe our reports to the typing pool. And we grew up without fax machines.

The advent of email forced many of us to confront the internet and personal computing out of necessity, but we still did not learn much besides turning on the power and hand pecking our emails, and turning the computer off and back on when it got stuck.

The younger generations and our grandkids today arrive out of the womb carrying their mobile handheld PDA personal digital assistant computers in their tiny hands and seemingly come preprogrammed with natural computer skills absorbed in-utero from their intelligent mothers who are keyboarding nightly on their own computers while the grandkids are still in gestation.

Fortunately for us the keyboarding skills needed to self-publish your own book today are greatly reduced. You will use the sophisticated easy to use computer interfaces programmed into today's generation of powerful smart computer software designed by these clever Boomer and X generation kids we parented into this world and to whom we gave roots and wings. They have returned their thanks by publishing incredibly sophisticated and easy to use software, building on the WYSIWYG *"What you See is What You Get"* interfaces that hide complex programming and enable us older folks to produce great results needing only basic keyboarding skills.

The old hunt and peck two fingered approach and your mouse will work fine, just be patient, go step by step, and do not get intimidated. And if you really bog down and get stuck, you can always call the grandkids to help you out. What a wonderful way to involve your own progeny (one time removed) to get yourself involved in their lives and to have them involved in documenting yours.

Technology comes seemingly second nature to the young. Our two young grandchildren have an iPad-mini and a Kindle-Fire we gave them. Upon opening her gift, our little granddaughter quickly figured it out on her own, hooked up to the internet using the wireless router in their home, did a Google search, and proudly played us a variety of pre-recorded "fart" sounds from some distant web site. Grandma and Grandpa almost died laughing. Her parents were not pleased.

And now just this morning, two years older, she came to me in my office and asked if I had *"a spare USB port she could use to charge up her Dad's iPad"* to supplement library books from school so she and her brother could do their half hour of reading early each morning before the family wakes up and gets going.

Whatever it takes to get familiar with use of the new technology builds competency and confidence. We provide a credit card account for each of the grandchildren to be able to download their own eBooks to encourage reading, knowing that some of the credit would probably be used for electronic games which themselves build familiarity and interaction with the electronic reading device.   JL

8-d) Mental acuity as we age:

Over the years I have observed there are generally two types of people in the world, Chickens and Owls. Chickens go to bed early and wake up early and alert. Owls go to bed late (take a long time to settle into sleep), and they wake up late and slowly in the morning, taking a long time to fully arouse and become engaged and alert.

And I have noticed another almost irrefutable law of nature. In many successful long time marriages, Chickens marry Owls and vice versa. That is the case for Karen and me. I get into bed, pull up the covers, and as my head approaches the pillow, like a "Kewpie" doll my eyes start to close and Karen tells me by the time my head hits the pillow I am fully asleep, sleeping the sleep of the innocent, not to move until a precise time in the morning, always close to 6am, when I awake and jump out of bed alert, refreshed and 100% ready to go.

On the other hand, the last thing I see each night is Karen on her side of the bed, ear phones on and watching the silent TV with her book or Kindle in her hands and her small night-light focusing the light on her reading. And then a long 1-2 hour slow decent into sleep.

Then reversed in the morning, she suffers a long slow reentry into the world and is semi-comatose and almost worthless until I deliver her a large hot cup of strong steaming Swedish coffee in bed along with a sweet bite to eat and the morning newspapers.

Karen's sewing room shelves are full of books as are the shelves of our family room and our closets and our cars. Her Kindle is loaded almost to capacity with other books. She surrounds herself with books. She self contentedly quoted to me an article in the paper just recently that **intellectual pursuits including reading (and publishing) books are key to maintaining mental acuity as the years move on**. I married a very smart lady.   JL

---

9) Self-publishing your own book is a supreme mental acuity exercise:

So get yourself started. At our age, our time is mostly our own now and we have a lot of time to self-indulge. One of those self-indulgences should be to self-publish your own book. It is never too late to get started.

Actually that is not entirely true. I publish the *In Memoriam* section of our *Punahou Class of 1959* and our *Yale Class of 1963* web sites and post the obituaries and remembrances of classmates recently departed.

The continually growing list reminds us that time marches on, our time here is NOT unlimited, and that getting started earlier rather than later is probably a good idea.

The recently published books of my classmates including William Nordhaus - *The Climate Casino: Risk, Uncertainty, and Economics for a Warming World,* David Boren - *A Letter to America,* and John Lahr - *Tennessee Williams: Mad Pilgrimage of the Flesh,* are indeed testaments that our peak mental acuity and ability to produce important and relevant books are still ahead of us. JL

---

10) Hire an Editor:
My suggestions to authors:
   a) Hire an editor.
   b) Check out PCIP *Quality Books Inc* . http://www.quality-books.com/pcip.htm   This is one type of cataloging in publication. Do a P-CIP.
   c) Get five prepublication reviews. Use a mockup edition.   JS

---

11) The Library of Congress Control Number – LCCN:

If you plan to make your book available to libraries, you should obtain a Library of Congress Control Number, or LCCN, so your book is given a unique identifier and is eligible for library cataloging nationwide. The LCCN is a serially based system of numbering and cataloging records in the Library of Congress in the United States. It has nothing to do with the contents of any book and should not be confused with Library of

Congress Classification. The LCCN must be assigned before your first publication. It will carry through for all future versions of your book regardless of print format; hardcover, softcover, and eBook.

Libraries use the Library of Congress database in addition to other databases to stay up-to-date on available titles. Make it easier for them to purchase your book by registering for a Library of Congress Control Number (LCCN), a unique identification number that the Library of Congress assigns and uses for cataloging and other book-processing activities.

The purpose of the Preassigned Control Number (PCN) program is to enable the Library of Congress to assign control numbers in advance of publication to those titles that may be added to the Library's collections. The publisher prints the control number in the book and thereby facilitates cataloging and other book processing activities. The PCN links the book to any record which the Library of Congress, other libraries, bibliographic utilities, or book vendors may create.

This is a two-step process. All publishers wanting to participate in the PCN Program must first complete and submit an Application to Participate. When the application has been approved, an account number and password will be sent to the publisher via email. Then, publishers participating in the program logon to the PCN system and complete a Pre-assigned Control Number Application Form for each title for which a pre-assigned control number is requested. Based on the information provided by the publisher, Library staff pre-assign a control number to each eligible title. Upon receiving the number, the publisher prints it on the back of the title page (i.e., the copyright page) in the following manner:

The Library of Congress Control Number for this book: 2014906294. The LCCN numbering system has been in use since 1898, at which time the acronym LCCN originally stood for Library of Congress Card Number. It has also been called the Library of Congress Catalog Card Number, among other names. The Library of Congress prepared cards of bibliographic information for their library catalog and would sell duplicate sets of the cards to other libraries for use in their catalogs. This is known as centralized cataloging. Each set of cards was given a serial number to help identify it.

Although most of the bibliographic information is now electronically created, stored and shared with other libraries, there is still a need to identify each unique record, and the LCCN continues to perform that function. Librarians all over the world use this unique identifier in the process of cataloging most books which have been published in the United States. It helps them reach the correct cataloging data (known as a cataloging record), which the Library of Congress and third parties make available on the Web and through other media.

In February 2008, the Library of Congress created the LCCN Permalink service, providing a stable URL for all Library of Congress Control Numbers.

There are two methods to get your LCCN:

1- Your publisher can get this number for you for a moderate fee, typically close to $50.00.

2- Do it yourself: The LCCN **is** free and can be obtained in 1-2 weeks.

http://www.loc.gov/publish/pcn/newaccount.html

If you have an account already, the "**EPCN Login**" button brings you to the form requiring your Account ID and Password. Fill out and click on the "**Sign On**" button and fill out the form. You will be required to transmit a complete copy of your book in ASCII format, and then a copy of your completed book once published. Your LCCN will come to you via email.

We recommend paying for the service your first time and have your publisher do it for you. We had CreateSpace do it for us for $49.00 in five days. We inserted it into the copyright page.

This same LCCN will be good for all future versions of this book unless the format is changed (from casebound hardcopy to softcopy), for which each different form will require a new LCCN. eBooks are ineligible for an LCCN, even though their print version counterpart may have one

To apply for an LCCN you must already have your unique ISBN which is assigned by your software vendor when the book is first created. JL

12) P-CIP - Publishers Cataloging In Publication:

Solo self-publishers cannot get a CIP, but we include this information for your edification in the event you move on to be massively successful and libraries and book stores around the world want to stock your books on their shelves.

Librarians require much more specific information about new titles to facilitate the acquisition and processing of those titles, including the determination of the exact shelf location for the materials within the library.

The purpose of Cataloging In Publication (CIP) is to provide librarians with all the information they need, in an agreed-upon format and vocabulary, prior to the time that full cataloging is available.

If you plan to market your book to libraries, you should include CIP on the title page verso of your publication. While it's not intended to be a marketing tool, it can help to sell your product to libraries.

CIP--The Two Types

There are two types of Cataloging In Publication:

 LC-CIP, for which the cataloging is prepared by the Library of Congress (LC), and

P-CIP, for which the cataloging information is prepared by the publisher or his/her agent (i.e., Quality Books Inc.)

Although the Library of Congress provides CIP's for well over 50,000 books per year, they cannot begin to process all of the requests for CIP's that they receive. 80% of the publishers in the LC CIP program are small publishers meaning they produce 10 or fewer titles a year.

Visit the CIP web site: http://www.loc.gov/publish/cip/

A Cataloging in Publication record (aka CIP data) is a bibliographic record prepared by the Library of Congress for a book that has not yet been published. When the book is published, the publisher includes the CIP data on the copyright page thereby facilitating book processing for libraries and book dealers.

Purpose of the CIP Program

- The purpose of the Cataloging in Publication (CIP) Program is to serve the nation's libraries by cataloging books in advance of publication.
- Publishers submit applications via the Library of Congress Web site.
- The Library creates a bibliographic record for each publication and sends it to the publisher.
- The publisher prints the record (known as CIP data) on the verso of the title page.
- The CIP data is thereby available to each library that acquires a copy of the book.
- The Library of Congress also distributes these records weekly in machine readable form to large libraries, bibliographic services, and book vendors around the world.
- Many of these organizations redistribute these records in products and services designed to alert the library community to forthcoming publications and to facilitate acquisition.

There is no need to worry about getting a CIP at this point, assuming you are still learning the ropes, that this is your first book, and that you expect to sell your book initially through one of the online publishing services as Amazon.com or as an eBook over the Internet. JL

13) Formatting and editing:

This book assumes you already have a fully completed and edited manuscript ready to submit for publishing. After collecting and organizing the content of your book and composing it all into organized text, getting a document 100% composed to convert into a publishable book is another daunting challenge involving:

1. General layout and organization of the sections
2. Pagination
3. Header and footer labeling
4. Insertion of fleurons
5. Ordering of standard sections
6. Title page and Copyright/Publishing details
7. Table of Contents
8. Preface / Introduction
9. Chapters
10. References / Notes section / Bibliography
11. Index

If you choose to prepare your own document using a word processor, it will take certain skills to be developed. I keyboarded this entire document myself into publishable form using Microsoft Word 2007. In spite of my considerable typing skills acquired over many years at IBM and since and heretofore extensive use of and familiarity with Word 2007, I had to invest time into learning the techniques for composition of pagination, sectioning, and header and footer labeling. If you do not possess these skills, you will need to use a Template or find someone to keyboard all of your material into the fairly standard form required by the publisher.

In the Appendix you will see a section on Formatting your manuscript to get it into the condition required by any self-publishing company including the important Copyright verso page on the back of the Title Page.

In our Yale 1963 days, we keyed our own papers and reports on manual typewriters using erasable onion paper, or liquid white-out to cover keyed errors for retyping. In some cases we hired professional typists who would transcribe our handwritten document on a typewriter, who charged by the word and by the page. And then we had to deal with the old Ampeco (*American Photocopy Equipment Company*) duplicating machines for making copies that always smelled like the alcohol used in the purple ink.

Our papers were printed in two type sizes, Pica or Elite (10 or 12 characters per inch), with only a single font (Courier). Boldface involved backing up the carriage and retyping the same sequence two or three times. The IBM Selectric-II revolutionized typing with its insertable type ball allowing different fonts and auto-correcting that backed up the carriage and inserted the white out ribbon for you as you retyped the correction. Introduced in 1961 they were too rare and expensive at $600 apiece for us college kids.

The Xerox 914, introduced in 1959, the year I graduated high school and entered college, was not in common use. Billed as the "the most successful single product of all time," the 914, was the first plain paper photocopier. Early investors became millionaires.

My grandfather Hadley chose earlier to invest a good portion of my inheritance from him to be used towards my college education, in the form of Ampeco stock. Ampeco lost the race and failed/disappeared after the Xerox process and success, leaving me having to earn a living rather than retiring early on the investment. Had he put the $20,000 into *The Haloid Photographic Company*, the precursor to Xerox, that $20,000 would have been $2 million by the time I graduated in 1963 which was the year Xerox introduced the Xerox 813, the first desktop plain-paper copier, a copier that could fit on anyone's office desk. But enough history.

Recommendation: Unless you are a good keyboarder and are willing to learn some new tricks about pagination, sectioning, and header and footer formatting, you had best find yourself a good keyboarder, someone to key your book for you. Or use a good template. Or find a full service self-publishing company who will accept manuscripts and convert them for a fixed price, like Bookstand Publishing.   JL

---

14) "Why do you want to Publish?"

Publishing is changing so rapidly that it is increasingly futile to ask "How To" publish your book. To me, the important questions are:

(1) Why do you want to publish?
- (a) You have something you want to say,
- (b) You want to leave a bit of you for others,
- (c) Other,
- (d) You hope to make money.

If your answer to (1) is (a), (b), or maybe (c), then

(2) Who is your audience?
> (a) friends,
> (b) colleagues,
> (c) general audience

If your answer to (2) is (a) or (b), then an ISBN is optional.

If your answer to (1) is (d), **you will have to market your book**, and you will have to do it by yourself.

Unless you are a really best-selling author, even publishing houses don't provide much help. To market, including having readings at book shops, a "platform"- (blog, website, or social media coverage) is essential. You will not get a public reading without one because the venue wants to be sure that people will show up.

I believe perhaps the least expensive place to have your book printed - is Publishers Graphics   http://www.pubgraphics.com/. They do the actual printing for many self-publishing companies. They charge about $2.00 less per book and do very good work.   RF

---

15) Skill, luck, timing, persistence, and starting small:

I was bitten by the muse early and served as poetry editor of our high school literary magazine and wrote feature articles for the school newspaper. I didn't write at Yale or really again until middle age. After college I went to medical school, got a Ph.D. in biochemistry and began a career as a research physician. In midlife the muse elbowed her way into my psyche again and threatened to overwhelm my professional life.

To make a long story short, to be successful as a published author, it's best to be young, tall, good-looking with a full head of hair, have a commanding presence and a stentorian voice. (Having a supportive wife who has written eight well-received books of non-fiction is a huge asset.) Failing these, **to find a publisher, luck and the kindness of strangers are essential**. And I've had plenty of both.

I was giving a poetry reading one night in Houston almost twenty-five years ago, and afterward a guy who ran a small press came up and asked if I would like him to publish a book of my poetry—a once in a million occurrence, rarer than...well, the second coming, *Birnam Wood's coming to* Dunsinane, or dancing termites gnawing at Captain

Hook's wooden arm. I was exceptionally lucky when my poems won a Texas Review Press contest for publication of a first book of poems. And so it went with my six books of poems. All have been published by small presses, which, considering I had a day job with a large research lab and a department to chair, made me feel extraordinarily lucky. And if they weren't Random House or FSG, or Knopf, I hardly cared.

When I set out to publish my first novel, _Never Surrender-Never Retreat, A Novel of Medical Politics in Texas,_ rather than looking for an agent and hoping she could place the book (at age seventy an iffy proposition), I went to Texas Review Press—Sam Houston State University's press—and shopped it directly. Again, good fortune—they took it. I've stuck with them for two additional novels—_The Lobsterman's Daughter_ and _The Women of Harvard Square, A Novel in Short Stories_—both due out in 2014.

To find a publisher, the only two things I can recommend are:

1) **Work hard at the craft of writing** (some passages have been rewritten twenty or thirty times) and **be persistent**.

2) **Meeting people** and **luck** give you some chance of success.
And I am one lucky S.O.B.   ML

Start small and be Opportunistic: My book was published and printed in Saigon by a government-owned press. My subject is a very famous combat artist during the Vietnam War. He, like most Viet Cong guerillas, spent years in the jungle base camps, where an insurgent bureaucracy was hidden, and this included a primitive print shop where propaganda leaflets and training manuals were printed on truly antique presses. After the South was overrun and Vietnam was reunified in 1975, his colleagues who ran the Viet Cong print shop in the jungle set up a tiny printing business in the now-peaceful Saigon. By the time I finished my book in 2006, Saigon had become a dynamic metropolis, and the small ex-Viet Cong print shop had become Saigon's biggest and most modern printer, with German-made high-speed color presses.

The management of the business, wartime veterans and colleagues of the artist about whom I wrote, were eager to honor their famous friend, and so they provided all the technical support and did the printing and binding all at a nominal cost. I was very lucky. I certainly don't anticipate that happening again in my lifetime!   LK

16) Why Self-Publish?

In the future, Self-publishing skills will be an essential element of (y)our success.

The advent of the Internet brought us:
- Instant email,
- Online news services,
- Video services as YouTube allowing sharing of video content worldwide almost as soon as events transpire,
- Handheld mobile personal content viewing platforms,
- Digital books delivered immediately and read online,
- Instant sharing of personal news/photos via social networks.

Today, estimates project that worldwide:
- 2.4 billion people (1 in 3 in the world) access the Internet.
- There are now over 2.4 billion web pages
- On over 110 million web sites.
- Apple has sold over 200 million IPads.

Cisco predicts that the number of network-connected devices will be more than 15 billion, twice the world's population, by 2015. In the fifth annual Cisco® Visual Networking Index (VNI) Forecast (2010-2015), the company also said the total amount of global Internet traffic will quadruple by 2015 and reach 966 exabytes per year.

   The projected increase of Internet traffic between 2014 and 2015 alone is 200 exabytes, which is greater than the total amount of Internet Protocol traffic generated globally in 2010. On the verge of reaching one zettabyte, which is equal to a sextillion bytes, or a trillion gigabytes by 2015, global IP traffic growth is driven by four primary factors, according to Cisco.

-1 An increasing number of devices: The proliferation of tablets, mobile phones, connected appliances and other smart machines is driving up the demand for connectivity. By 2015, there will be nearly 15 billion network connections via devices -- including machine-to-machine -- and more than two connections for each person on earth.

-2 More Internet users: By 2015, there will be nearly 3 billion Internet users -- more than 40 percent of the world's projected population.

-3 Faster broadband speed: The average fixed broadband speed is expected to increase four-fold, from 7 megabits per second in 2010 to 28 Mbps in 2015. The average broadband speed has already doubled within the past year from 3.5 Mbps to 7 Mbps.

-4 More video: By 2015,one million video minutes --the equivalent of 674 days --will traverse the Internet every second.

And now with the advent of low cost easy to use self-publishing tools, individuals are able to create content and to put it out to the world for mass consumption. This will drastically increase the amount of information available to us to be read and consumed, at lower costs.

There will never be a substitute for sitting in a comfortable chair at home browsing through a physical book, turning the pages, turning page corners on good sections, and hi-light marking key sentences. We hope this pleasure is never taken from us, it is one of life's great pleasures.

But to keep up with a fast paced world, downloading larger amounts of lower cost books in digital form and browsing them on our handheld Personal Digital Assistants will be required to keep up. JL

---

17) Technology in the classrooms: On a parallel with the self-publishing technologies presented in this book, huge strides are also being made using **technology in the classrooms** for high school and colleges and universities including:

-1) Turning the classroom around with the teachers and professors self-videoing their lectures which students watch at home in the evening and then do their homework in the classroom, joint learning in teams, with the teacher's direct assistance.

- 2) Full online courses taken at home over the Internet. Accessing Yale's *Openyalecourses.com*, I am digesting as many free online courses as I can, making up for the formal Yale classroom time of my liberal arts roommates that I missed while studying electrical engineering and industrial administration.

Coursera: *https://www.coursera.org/* is an education platform that partners with top universities and organizations worldwide to offer courses online for anyone to take, for free. *Coursera* envisions a future where everyone has access to a world-class education. *Coursera* aims to empower people with education that will improve their lives, the lives of their families, and the communities in which they live. Former 20 year Yale University President Richard C. ("Rick") Levin is the new CEO of the company.

This subject (*technology in the classroom*) is beyond the scope of this book which focuses on self-publishing. But **the two fields (classroom technology and publishing technology) will merge in the future** as we find ourselves writing courses for our own material to be self-learned by others in conjunction with classroom teaching.

Our old home of almost 40 years here in Tiburon is in transition. It is filled with books. But we are converting to digital reading. I go to sleep every night with Karen huddled up with her Kindle in bed next to me where she can silently download a new book over our in-home wireless network and then page silently through it as I sleep. But she still prefers the hardcover book and belongs to Book clubs who deliver through the mail. And we always have 3-4 books stashed in our cars so she has something to read while I am off running errands.

Our generation has one foot in the old manual book world and one in the new digital world. At times it is almost too easy to deal exclusively with electronic digital content. The older generation appreciates the world in which we grew up, favoring the slower physical book form. Our shelves at home are full of books, purchased, read once or twice, reread, and then revisited for the color coded hi-lights on occasion. Some of them eventually get donated to the local libraries to make room on our shelves for new books and to share our old books with others.

More and more content is now available for viewing on the Internet with more being created every day. It is virtually impossible for individuals to keep up with the explosion of new information.

Today people seem more anxious to broadcast information to others than to want to listen to and absorb information from and about others. As more and more content is generated, less and less of it is being read and studied. There just is not enough time each day to digest it all. So the onus is on self-publishers to generate books of highest quality. Quality over quantity must remain our primary objective.   JL

---

18) Profit potential from Self-Publishing:

If you are publishing only to make money, you will most likely fail. However, a good knowledge of the costs and potential profits to you for your work are necessary and helpful in determining your budget to produce your book and the potential earnings if you are successful.

Based on my own experience, it is my belief that using this guide, you can successfully:
- Self-publish your own book,
- In softcover format,
- In 7-14 days elapsed,
- At minimal cost to you.

(under $100.00 for the LCCN number and ten softcover copies mailed to your home) assuming you have medium computer keyboarding skills and do not retain any of the optional consulting services.

Cost Details:
1- Total cost for this first trade book production was **$95.00**.
($49.00 for the LCCN Library of Congress Control Number, $7.00 for the initial prototype proof softcopy for final review, plus $39.00 for

the first ten softcopy books mailed to my home). This first book is the result.

2- The total cost to then convert my book into a Kindle eBook available over the Internet online was an additional **$79.00**.

3- The cost to produce ten copies of the follow on hardcover b/w book was **$273.00** ($99.00 one-time fee. $49.00 for the LCCN, plus $12.50 per 262 page book). This provided me ten promotional hardcover copies to give away including to Yale, Punahou, Arcadia, Mill Valley and Tiburon libraries, and several vanity copies for myself.

Cost Summary: The total cost to self-publish and produce ten softcover copies of this book, register the book in the U.S. Library of Congress, buy one test proof, buy ten more softcopies for my friends, buy ten b/w hardcover books for distribution to libraries, and submit the color version of this book for online publishing as an eBook, was:

$ 49.00	LCCN number
$ 7.00	Softcover proof delivered to my home
$ 39.00	Ten softcover books delivered to my home
$273.00	Ten hardcover books for gifting to libraries
$ 79.00	Submit for online color distribution as an eBook
$ 447.00	Total cost

The Amazon.com and CreateSpace costs will vary. Below are the typical costs and expected profit levels for:
      1) the trade book softcover and
      2) the eBook online version for this book.

See the Appendix for book pricing to *Maximize your Royalties*.
1) **The black and white (with color cover) softcover trade book** version of this book is available for $18.00 on Amazon.com. The cost to produce (print and bind) black and white books is around $0.015 per page so this 262 page book costs around $4.00 to produce. After the $4.00 cost to produce is taken out, the remaining $14.00 royalty is split 50/50 with CreateSpace/Amazon.com and myself. I get est. $7.00 per book sold (50% of $14.00). The customer pays the shipping cost of course. These royalty split rates differ amongst various vendors.
Often a distributor will discount its royalty share of the published list price to encourage sales, reducing its royalty share from say 20% down

to 5-10%. This book is listed at my full list price of $18.00, but it can be purchased on Amazon.com currently for just under $16.00 with Amazon.com's discount. 3rd party distributors are offering it in the $12.00 to $15.00 range, reducing my royalty share to est. $3.50.

2) **The EBook version is also available on Kindle online**.

For online Kindle books, there is no production cost charged for the electronic delivery over the Internet. The royalty from the sale is split 30% to Kindle/CreateSpace and 70% to the Author. **My $9.99 Kindle eBook version** will net my 501(c)(3) *Larson Family Foundation* and my Yale 1963 class 70% x $9.99 less est. $0.30 electronic delivery **= $6.70 profit per book sold** which will be paid into my bank account automatically upon each sale since I signed up for the auto-pay feature. Otherwise Amazon will accumulate sales and will snail mail me a check monthly provided the amount exceeds $100.00.

My $447.00 total cost to publish this book can be recovered from the sale of $447.00 / $7.00 = 65 softcover or $447.00 / $6.70 = 67 eBooks. And then it is 100% profit after that as I sit back and watch the book sales take off. Ka ching! (we hope!) 1,000 softback copies sold nets $7.000. 10,000 copies sold nets $70,000. 100,000 copies sold ….. you do the math. We could eventually be talking some serious money here. And you only need to sell less than 100 books to recover your full development costs. JL

---

19) Using Professional Consulting services:

A full range of consulting services is available to assist you should you lack the essential keyboarding experience of people like myself who have been keyboarding since starting employment with IBM in 1967 and to whom desktop word processing is second nature.

CreateSpace does not provide for production of the required initial document in electronic format. Typing, transcription or ghost writing services must be obtained elsewhere. You can submit your book in rough keyed-in form as a simple text document with no formatting.

Basic line editing for spelling, grammar and context costs $0.016 per word. This 262 page book consists of close to 55,000 words so it would cost 55,000 x $0.16 = **$880.00** estimate for a full guaranteed Basic edit. This will give you a fully edited book.

Comprehensive developmental content editing is available typically for $0.021 per word, so it would cost an additional 55,000 x $0.021 = **$1,150.00** to have a consultant do a full edit of this book to include chapter design, formatting, indexing, contents, pagination, font design, and context formatting.

Custom design of a full cover front and back with title, book description, author description, images, and creative artwork could typically cost an additional estimated **$600.00** or more.

You could pay **a total of $2,630** in consulting fees to take a rough text document in electronic form and have it fully prepared as input to a Self-Publishing system. This is still a very good bargain these days considering the effort it takes and the specialized skills to turn out a professional looking document that is 100% accurate.

Cost estimate Summary:
$ 880.00   Basic line editing consultant
$1,150.00   Comprehensive content editing consultant
$ 600.00   Cover design consultant
$ 447.00   Self-publishing cost: (2 LCCN's, one softcover proof,
                          10 softcover b/w books,10 hardcover b/w
                          books, and full color eBook distribution)
$3,077.00   est. Total cost to publish

Companies that offer publishing consulting services like CreateSpace will relate sales figures from their experience that show that books prepared by professional consulting staff have a sales rate long term of 2-3 times the amateur prepared books. It will take sales of 450 softcover copies of a typical book resembling this one at a $7.00 profit each to recover the full initial production cost including full consulting services to produce a professional book for you. The additional cost will greatly increase the odds you will be successful. JL

20) It can be Easy:

In my case, I have never self-published. I suspect as with many of the books in our list, the publisher, (in our case Elsevier), wined and dined my co-author and I to persuade us to produce these four volumes. They took care of all the rest and send us yearly royalty checks. ED note: This is an Author's ideal dream situation, having a Publisher approach you. You and your material must be unique and determined to be significant, and unless you have previously published, you need to have an established reputation in your profession

---

21) Hiring experts to help you Self-Publish:

In publishing *The Art of Japanese Cloisonné Enamel: History, Techniques and Masters, 1600 to the Present,* I strongly preferred not to self or author-financed publish. I faced a handicap in finding a publisher because I lacked what many publishers (particularly university presses) of scholarly books greatly prefer, that is, to publish well-known scholars having the appropriate Ph.D. degree and a prestigious university chair or museum curatorial position. In addition, a visual art book that requires color images is more expensive to produce than pure text. Despite credentials as a lecturer in my field and a board member of a related national art society, no university publisher was interested.

I was aware, however, that the academic Association for Asian Studies (AAS) holds an annual conference at which many publishers operate booths in order to both sell their wares and find new books to publish. I attended armed with an extensive summary sheet describing the book and my background, plus a five-page table of contents, and discussed these with dozens of publishers, including author-financed, university, and trade. Author-financed publishing did not suit me.

The most important Japanese-culture trade publisher offered to publish my book and wanted to include even more full-page color photos than I anticipated, which I would have been delighted to do, but they also insisted that I reduce the scholarly text by one-third in order to enable them to produce the book with a list price of $75. Because my goal in writing the book was to publish the detailed information and interpretive material in my text, rather than to produce a pictureBook, I decided to forego the prestige and wider sales that this publisher offered. I was fortunate at AAS to also meet McFarland & Company, Inc., a publisher that produces 200 or 300 scholarly or reference books a year.

I found working with McFarland comparatively easy. I am pleased that the company is privately owned in North Carolina and does all its work, including printing, in the United States. There are drawbacks, however; overall, their book design was more efficient than attractive, a problem particularly important for an art history dependent on images. Also, they made it clear to me that they were not a trade publisher, so that their distribution would be limited to institutional customers; this and their stringent rules limiting discounts and trade terms have meant that I have had to do most of the marketing for the book or rely on word of mouth for publicity and sales.

Self-publishing has increasingly become an ever more practical and widespread option. Moreover, **the author undoubtedly receives a larger percentage of the self-publishing sales price than his royalty from a publisher.** So self-publishing seems to me a viable alternative for those interested in doing it. I strongly suggest, however, that **an author pursuing this alternative should utilize the services of a book designer and a copy editor.**   FS

---

22) Good writing always comes at a premium:

In today's wired world with social media recording and reporting our every move, the many benefits of speed and lower cost of the digital format can come at a price if we allow ourselves to engage our fingers and our eyes, but leave our brains and hearts behind.

The best writing most often begins patiently in an empathetic heart that is in tune with the needs and feelings of others and the world around us, and then works its way into the brain, and only then to the eyes and fingers, and finally through the printed media into the world. The mouthpiece should be last in line in the process, not the first.

The reverse sequence seems to rule too much of our lives today. Too often today communication begins with the mouth first, and then is relayed in the digital media through the fingers and the eyes, and perhaps then engages the brain while often bypassing the empathetic heart completely.

With technology today, the process of getting information out into the world has accelerated to the point where we are compromising quality for speed and quantity. We hope and expect that the new generation of earnest self-publishers will take this into consideration and will make certain that we are producing high quality and valuable content for as wide an audience as possible, for the highest good.   JL

---

23) Producers and Critics...

From my experience studying human archetypes, one overly simplified observation is that there are basically two types of people in this world, **Producers** and **Critics**.
    -**Producers** produce real stuff.
    -**Critics** produce criticism of stuff produced by the Producers.

The Producer says "**Let me show you**." The Critic says *"**Show me!**"*

<u>Merriam-Webster dictionary</u> **definitions:**

pro·duc·er   *noun* \prə-ˈdü-sər, prō-, -ˈdyü-\
-Someone who is in charge of making and usually providing the money for a play, movie, record, (book), etc.
- Someone or something that grows or makes particular goods or products.
Full Definition of *PRODUCER*
1 : One that produces; *especially* : one that grows agricultural products or manufactures crude materials into **articles of use.**
2 : A person who supervises or finances a work (as a staged or recorded performance) for exhibition or dissemination to the public.

crit·ic   *noun* \ˈkri-tik\
1 *a* : One who expresses a reasoned opinion on any matter especially involving a judgment of its value, truth, righteousness, beauty, or technique.
1 *b* : One who engages often professionally in the analysis, evaluation, or appreciation of works of art or artistic performances.

2 : One given to **harsh or captious judgment.**

It does seem that our country currently is favoring the Critics. More and more of us are focused on criticizing the work of others while a seeming minority of folks are working to produce "real stuff" that enriches the lives of themselves and others and provides fodder to keep the critics busy.

Many of us today are concerned that our great country is:
1) Creating minimal new real wealth,
2) Focused on creating paper assets (making money with money),
3) Redistributing (leveling) the existing wealth that has been produced over 250 years rather than producing significant new real wealth.

This plays out in our politics. In its most extreme interpretation, conservatives believe they produce the wealth and that liberals want to take the wealth away from those who produce it and redistribute/share it with the non-producers. Producers and Critics? Who is to say? Risking over-simplification, my personal sense is that we are genetically predetermined to favor one archetype or the other, and that the general population of the human race is split 50/50 between the two archetype predispositions. I am researching this subject using the writings of a number of published Authors including:

Carl Jung: *Memories, Dreams, Reflections*
Extroverted (Producer) and introverted (Critic) personality archetypes and the collective unconscious.

Helen Palmer: *The Enneagram: Understanding Yourself and the Others In Your Life*   The Nine points of the Enneagram:
-Reformer, - Helper, -Motivator (*Producer*), -Romantic, -Thinker, -Skeptic (*Critic*), -Enthusiast,- Leader, and -Peacemaker.

Cris Evatt: *The Givers and the Takers*
Everyone is more of a Giver (*Producer*) or a Taker (*Critic*). A Giver-Taker (*producer/critic*) imbalance exists to some degree in most close relationships: romantic relationships, parent-child relationships, friendships and co-worker relationships.

Jean Shinoda Bolen:
Gods in Everyman: Archetypes that Shape Men's Lives
Goddesses in Everywoman: Powerful Archetypes in Women's Lives

Eight powerful inner patterns--or archetypes--that shape men's personalities, careers, and personal relationships. .... eight archetypal gods, or personality types, from the authoritarian power-seeking gods (Zeus, Poseidon) to the gods of creativity (Apollo, Hephaestus) to the sensual Dionysus. And the seven archetypal goddesses, or personality types, with whom all women can identify, from the autonomous Artemis and the cool Athena to the nurturing Demeter and the creative Aphrodite.

David Bruce Cornay: *Eros and Nihilism: Studies in the Possibility of a Human World* focuses on the two main opposing forces in human existence--the erotic, **creative** (Producer) force behind our construction of a world, versus the nihilistic, destructive force (Critic) directed toward nothingness.

All of these books are available electronically online now as eBooks at a considerable discount from the cost of hardcopy books I purchased years ago. I still prefer hardcover or softcover books for research.

Part of the answer of course is for each of us to work to become more like the less dominant aspect of our personality (be it acquired or genetic). Producers need to learn to think more like Critics. And Critics need to learn to act more like Producers.

Critics need to acknowledge and become more respectful of and thankful for the contributions of the Producers, become less demanding that wealth be given to them (shared), enabling Producers to want to share more of their wealth voluntarily as they come to acknowledge "the needs of the shared Village" and the God-given benefits of the land and all of its people that are the basis of all wealth.

But what does this have to do with self-publishing?

This is a starting point and subject for a future (ninth) self-published book. I bring the subject up here to make the points that:

1) Self-Publishing allows controversial views like this proposed book subject I am now researching and plan to self-publish, to be presented for consideration and accepted, modified, or rejected by the world at large. This work will be available sooner, at minimal cost to me, in a low cost format, and easily accessible to a wide community of viewers, as a self-published book.

2) **Producers will love your work**, regardless. **Critics will not.** Don't' let the Critics beat you down or let fear of the Critics keep you from self-publishing. Listen to your fellow Producers including book Authors and self-publishers. They understand and will applaud your efforts, no matter how imperfect or misunderstood you may be.

From Pope's _Essay on Criticism,_ "_To err is human; to forgive, divine..._"

From my experience, Producers forgive often, quickly and easily.

As for Critics? Not so much! Seldom, and grudgingly.   JL

---

24) Self-publishing is here to stay...

Other than the role of eBooks in the publishing industry, nothing stokes the passion of bookies of every stripe (Meyer Lansky's ilk excluded) than self-publishing. Loved or loathed, it's here to stay. And done well, it's great.

First a little historical prospective: our greatest poet Walt Whitman self-published _Leaves of Grass_. Not only did he set the type, he wrote his own reviews, sent out promo copies (the one to Emerson is the most famous), and remained his own best promoter.

Like everything else, from bit coins to YouTube do-it-yourself videos, to creating your own photo album online, to global warming, **self-published fiction, nonfiction, and poetry are here to stay.**

The book market, like every other market, is a messy, unruly, unpredictable affair with winners and losers. It involves luck (lots of it), imaginative marketing, and patience. BTW, the internet is your friend.

But it also involves good books: books that are imaginative, well written, well edited, proofread, and—oh, how I hate to mention this—**spell-checked.**

The independent small press world is a great place to be. Without it, talented writers might spend years simply trying to find an agent.

So, go ahead, break a leg, wait a decent period, and write your memoir: "_How I Broke My Leg and Broke Into Publishing_."   ML

Looking ahead:

In the near future, self-publishing will become almost as ubiquitous as email is today as people by the millions acquire the skills and techniques for self-publishing. I predict that self-publishing courses, paired with reading and writing courses, will soon be introduced into the curricula of high schools and colleges and will serve as huge motivators for students to master the now four skills (reading, writing 'rithmetic, and self-**publishing**).

Self-publishing skills are going to provide you with a huge advantage towards achieving success in the brave new digital driven and connected world of the future.

By reading this book and getting started today, you will enjoy a head start on the millions of self-publishers certain to follow. You are a world class expert in some area of human endeavor, knowing as much or more about one or more subjects than anyone else. The world needs to have your views and experience and findings documented in digital format in a book, readily accessible in hard back or softcover format available through libraries or the mail, or in digital eBook electronic format delivered through the Internet.

The future promises to be exciting. Here's wishing you all the best in your own exciting publishing adventures to come.

Tiburon, California

From the Authors

"We hope that relating our experiences over the years getting our books published, will encourage and help you and others to do the same."

Yale Class of 1963 - "Books by Class Authors"

Sterling Memorial Library - New Haven, CT

Yale Beinecke Rare Book and Manuscript Library

1963

About the Authors

<u>Notes:</u>

Appendix:

Grammar:

This book assumes that your grammar is 100% correct. Our generation (high school in the 1950's), was taught hard and fast rules by stern English teachers. I recall my Punahou 9th grade English teacher Ms. Dunstan in 1956, who passed in 1999 at age 95. I ran into her at her Arcadia retirement home in Honolulu in 1995, 40 years after being a student in her English class. At age 91 she not only remembered me well but recalled to me and to her assembled group of retired teachers that as her student, I had troublesome writing habits of *"dangling my participles"* and *"writing sentences that were too long."* I am reviewing this book very closely to make certain that I have not mistakenly dangled any participles for fear of upsetting Ms. Dunstan who expected perfect grammar because she felt it was the most important signature in life for a properly educated person. As a self-publisher, either you learned to write perfect grammar from dedicated English teachers like Ms. Dunstan, or you should retain professional assistance of an editor to help you. We can't help you here.

One of the best sources of help today is *Garner's Modern American Usage*, edited by Bryan Garner, a usage guide for contemporary American English. It covers issues of usage, pronunciation, style, distinctions among commonly confused words and phrases, and notes on how to prevent verbosity and obscurity. In addition, it contains essays about the English language.

Formatting:

There are many decisions and choices to make about formatting your book. Some are dictated by time tested hard and fast rules. And some are currently usual and customary rules which could become accepted hard rules over time based on use and efficiency for the best purpose. With self-publishing, you are free to choose most any formatting and style you prefer.

Formatting standards for publishing today are changing, particularly with the advent of the Internet and blogging and sophisticated text editors and word processors. Rules get adopted (and changed) over the years. Some commonly accepted rules are subjective, some are flexible, and some are rigid (until usage changes them).

If you use a Publisher, the company will provide many services for you to get your manuscript into the correct format for printing be it an online service or a full service Publisher of hardcover and softcover trade books. If you are self-publishing, this final responsibility rests 100% with you the Author. For a professional appearance for your book and to maximize the sales of your book, you will want to follow industry standards wherever possible.

This section purports to be a high level introduction to the subject of formatting your manuscript for publishing. We recommend you acquire one or several of the reference materials referred to herein for a much deeper study of this subject which is beyond the scope of this book which is taking your completed manuscript and getting it self-published quickly and inexpensively.

As far as printed (typed) text, Ms. Dunstan and her carefully coordinated lineage of English teachers all made us follow rules. These rules were also drilled into me in my high school typewriting class including:
- You always indent the first line of each paragraph by five spaces.
- You always end the sentence with two spaces between the period and the start of the next sentence.
- You always put a period inside the end of any sentence ending in a quote.
- Paragraphs must be an appropriate length, 6-7 sentences max.
- You should space your writing to register 10-12 words average per line.

The rules for publishing have been extended over the years to now cover a wider spectrum. We review here the general rules that apply in nine key areas covering formatting.
1. Font typeface
2. Font size
3. Paragraph separation
4. Paragraph indent
5. Paragraph length
6. Justification: (left, right, center or full)

7. Periods and quotation marks
8. Chapter/Section titling
9. Page numbering

1) Font Typeface:

There are literally hundreds of fonts available today included in today's word processing software packages. Here are 13 of the more common fonts used in self-published books today. Publishers will have additional special fonts that they recommend.

Sans-serif fonts:
Arial - Type font example
Calibri – Type font example
Optima – Type font example
Tahoma – Type font example
Verdana – Type font example

Serif fonts:
Book Antiqua – Type font example
Bookman – Type font example
Century Schoolbook – Type font example
Garamond – Type font example
Georgia – Type font example
Goudy Old Style - Type font example
Palatino Linotype – Type font example
Times New Roman – Type font example

The font and text size need to be consistent and clear. A decorative and unusual font may look great, but it's usually not a good choice for the entire text of a book as it is harder to read than plainer, traditional fonts. It is generally accepted that Serif typefaces are easier to read for a long period of time than sans-serif fonts (a serif is the little projection at the start and end of the letter). If your book is being viewed only on screen and not printed, then some argue that sans-serif is better rendered on a screen. Five of the more popular sans-serif fonts are listed above. This book is published in Calibri which is a sans-serif font, chosen because this book will be read both as a hardcover and softcover, and online as an eBook, and for me, Calibri is one of the fonts that reads well for all requirements.

2) Font size:

Choose a **font size** that suits the type of book that you are writing. The ultimate line length for readability is still around 12 words per line. Always aim at that number for the average. If you pick a book dimension of 6" x 9", once you pick your font type, this will determine the font size to achieve your goal of 10-12 words per page. If you set your typeface in 12 point which is best in terms of legibility, then your line length is determined for you. You should then alter your margins so that the line length at 12 pt is about 12 words on average. But your page size in combination with the margins you set will determine the exterior dimensions of your book, or vice versa. You will note above that each font type for the same font size will produce different length text which must be considered as well.

3) Paragraph separation:

Each separate subject or thought should have its own paragraph.

The purpose of paragraphs is to break up the text into manageable chunks for the reader, to add visual interest to the page, and to allow people to skim for the information they want. It will indicate to your reader which pieces of information go together and help them understand your thinking.

Here are the formats chosen generally for this book:
1) The subject header line is in boldface and larger font.
2) Insert a blank line between the subject header line and the first paragraph.
3) Do not indent the first line of the first paragraph after the header line.
4) Indent subsequent paragraphs if the logic is contiguous.
5) If you indent, do not put a blank line between paragraphs

Other formatting standards in use today include:
1) Do not indent any paragraph.
2) Separate paragraphs with a blank line.

4) Paragraph Indent:

Where subject headings are provided, they can be formatted in a larger font size (and boldface) for emphasis. Insert a blank line between the heading line and the first line of the paragraph immediately following the heading. And for the first paragraph after the heading line and at the top of a page, do not indent.

Using an indent to indicate a new paragraph is optional now, in fact in Britain it is common not to indent, preferring just to leave a line space between paragraphs instead. I mix the U.S. and British standards in this book. Also I do not indent a new paragraph starting at the top of a new page. To me, non-indent and line spacing between paragraphs is more readable for a technical reference book as this one.

5) Paragraph length:

Do not make paragraphs too long; they can vary between one single sentence and about 6-7 sentences before they become unwieldy.

6) Justification:

Of the four standards, Left, Right, Center and Full, Full is the one most often used for books today. It allows both the left and the right margin to be vertical straight, thereby improving the appearance and neatness of the page. Technical books today often use left justification to allow perfect spacing of each line which will be more precise, especially when numbered text, formulas and equations are included. The great majority of the books printed today use Full justification.

7) Periods, Commas, and Quotation Marks:

In the U.S., periods at the end of a sentence generally go inside the quotation mark, regardless of logic. Period.

Rule 1
Periods and commas always go inside quotation marks, even inside single quotes.

Examples: *The sign changed from "Walk," to "Don't Walk," to "Walk"*
again within 30 seconds. *She said, "Hurry up."*
She said, "He said, 'Hurry up.'"

Rule 2
The placement of question marks with quotes follows logic. If a
question is in quotation marks, the question mark should be placed
inside the quotation marks. Examples: *She asked, "Will you still be*
my friend?" *Do you agree with the saying, "All's fair in love and war"?*
Here the question is outside the quote.

Note: Only one ending punctuation mark is used with quotation
marks. Also, the stronger punctuation mark wins. Therefore, no period
after *war* is used.

Rule 3
When you have a question outside quoted material AND inside quoted
material, use only one question mark and place it inside the quotation
mark. Example: *Did she say, "May I go?"*

Rule 4
Use single quotation marks for quotes within quotes. Note that the
period goes inside all quote marks. Example: *He said, "Danea said, 'Do*
not treat me that way.'"

Rule 5
Use quotation marks to set off a direct quotation only.
Examples:
"When will you be here?" he asked.
He asked when you will be there.

Rule 6
Do not use quotation marks with quoted material that is more than
three lines in length.

Rule 7
When you are quoting something that has a spelling or grammar
mistake or presents material in a confusing way, insert the term *sic* in
italics and enclose it in brackets. *Sic* means, "This is the way the
original material was."

Example: *She wrote, "I would rather die then [sic] be seen wearing the same outfit as my sister."* Should be *than*, not *then*.

In England, Canada and countries with British influence, periods go inside or outside the quotation mark, depending on the logic. In this book, I mix the two standards for readability.

---

8) Different margins on right and left pages:

You need to leave a wide "gutter" margin at the center of the book binder for readability. This book uses 1.1" for the inside margin and 0.5" for the outside margin.

MS Word setup instructions for inside and outside margins:

1. On the ribbon (at the top of the screen), click on *Page Layout*

2. In the Page Setup tab, click on *Margins*

3. At the bottom of the menu that pops up, click on *Custom Margins...*

4. About half way down the dialog box that pops up, you'll see Multiple Pages. In the box, select *Mirror Margins*

5. At the top of the dialog box where you enter your margins, "Left" and "Right" have changed to "Inside" and "Outside."

Other word processors as Adobe and Pages use similar techniques.

---

9) Chapter/Section Titles:

There is flexibility here. One common method today is to print the title of the book on the top of the even numbered pages along with the page number, and print the name of the chapter and the page number on the odd numbered pages. Or the chapter name can be printed on the bottom of the page along with the page number. Well known authors writing novels will print their own name on the top of even numbered pages and the book title on the odd numbered pages. For this author, not being well known (at least not yet), we simply list the chapter/section title and the page number on the bottom of each page and leave the top of each page blank. And we start page numbering with 1 and skip the fancy roman numerals sometimes used in the introduction section.

---

10) Page Numbering:

Word processors will insert flexible page numbering any way you wish. It can be bottom centered, or left or right justified on the top of each page along with the book title or chapter name. In no case should you insert the text "Page" in front of each page number. Some books will use lower case roman numerals for the introduction, contents, and acknowledgments sections of the book and start numbering from 1 on the first chapter.

---

11) Sources of formatting documentation:

Here are some more sources for self-publishers:

How to Format Your Book for Self Publication
selfpublishingmadeeasy.wordpress.com

How to Format Your Self-Published Book
www.writing-world.com/publish/format.shtml

Self-Publish Your Book   BookStand Publishing:
www.bookstandpublishing.com/pod4/

For technical assistance with word processing:

Book Formatting for Self-Publishers, a Comprehensive How-To Guide: Easily Format Books with Microsoft Word; by Jennette Green

Book Formatting Tips by V Karen McMahon

How to Self-Publish Your Book Using Microsoft Word 2007: A Step-by-Step Guide for Designing & Formatting Your Book's Manuscript & Cover to PDF & POD Specifications, including those of CreateSpace. by Edwin Scroggins

---

12) Style guides:

Wikipedia is probably the best single source point to start to locate books and articles that will assist you to format the style (look and feel) of your book, depending on the audience and purpose of your book. Below I have copied freely from Wikipedia and give full credit for the material that follows to Wikipedia with the hope that the reader will pursue the links on your own and will make a donation to Wikipedia as I and my small 501(c)(3) foundation www.lff1.org have done. I intend to donate also from proceeds from this book. Wikipedia is a self-funded not-for-profit organization.

In the United States, most non-journalism writing follows *The Chicago Manual of Style*, while most newspapers base their style on the *Associated Press Stylebook*. A classic style guide for the general public is *The Elements of Style*.

For general writing:

- *The Careful Writer*, by Theodore Bernstein.
- *Bryson's Dictionary of Troublesome Words: A Writer's Guide to Getting It Right*, by Bill Bryson.
- *Garner's Modern American Usage* by Bryan A. Garner.
- *The Classics of Style* — presents writing guidance from William Strunk, Jr., Emerson, Whitman, Poe, and other writers.

- *The Elements of Style*. By William Strunk, Jr. and E. B. White. (often referred to as "Strunk and White")

For electronic publishing:

- *The Columbia Guide to Online Style*, by Janice Walker and Todd Taylor.
- *Web Style Guide: Basic Design Principles for Creating Web Sites,* by Patrick J. Lynch and Sarah Horton.

For business:

- *The Business Style Handbook, An A-to-Z Guide for Effective Writing on the Job*, by Helen Cunningham and Brenda Greene
- *The Gregg Reference Manual*, by William A. Sabin.

For the computer industry (software and hardware):

- *Apple Publications Style Guide* by Apple Inc. Provides editorial guidelines for text in Apple instructional publications, technical documentation, reference information, training programs, and the software user interface.
- *Microsoft Manual of Style for Technical Publications*, by Microsoft Corporation. Provides a style standard for technical documentation including use of terminology, conventions, procedure, design treatments, punctuation, and grammar usage.

Editorial style guides on preparing a manuscript for publication:

- *The Chicago Manual of Style*, by University of Chicago Press

A **style guide** or **style manual** is a set of standards for the writing and design of documents, either for general use or for a specific publication, organization or field. The implementation of a style guide provides uniformity in style and formatting within a document and across multiple documents.

For example, long novels with no images and pure text (like a romance or adventure or sci-fi novel that flows on for hundreds of pages), typically are full justified left and right, use a serif type font, indent each paragraph, and have no spaces between paragraphs. By contrast, a Microsoft user guide with diagrams, instructions, text, boldface headers and block inserts will typically be in a sans-serif type font, insert a line between paragraphs, left justify, and not indent.

A set of standards for a specific organization is often known as "house style." Style guides are common for general and specialized use, for the general reading and writing audience, and for students and scholars of various academic disciplines, medicine, journalism, the law, government, business, and industry.

Organizations advocating for social minorities sometimes establish what they believe to be fair and correct language treatment of their audiences.

Some style guides focus on graphic design, focusing on such topics as typography and white space. Web site style guides cover a publication's visual and technical aspects, along with text.

Many style guides are revised periodically to accommodate changes in conventions and usage. The *Associated Press Stylebook*, for example, is revised annually.

Style guides vary by country of publication and consumption audience.

1 International
2 Australia
3 Canada
4 United Kingdom
5 United States
    5.1 For general writing
    5.2 For legal documents
    5.3 For academic papers
    5.4 For journalism
    5.5 For electronic publishing
    5.6 For business
    5.7 For the computer industry (software and hardware)
    5.8 Editorial style guides on preparing a manuscript for publication

Some specific style guides:

ACS Style Guide, *AMA Manual of Style*, *Bluebook*. *The Chicago Manual of Style*, *The Elements of Typographic Style*, *ISO 690*, *The Microsoft Manual of Style*, *The New York Times Manual*, *The Oxford Guide to Style/New Hart's Rules*

---

13) Recto and Verso:

These are two words to add to your publishing vocabulary. They are used in the binding, printing, and publishing industries. The recto and verso are respectively the "front" and "back" sides of a leaf of paper in a bound book. In languages written from left to right (such as English) the recto is the right-hand page and the verso the left-hand page of an open book showing two pages (excepting some first pages).

Copyright page:

The required copyright page is located on the back side (verso) of the title page. This page carries the copyright notice, edition information, publication information, printing history, cataloging data, legal notices, the book's ISBN or identification number, the LCCN Library of Congress Control Number, and the P-CIP number of the publisher. Rows of numbers are sometimes printed at the bottom of the page to indicate the year and number of the printing. Credits for design, production, editing and illustration are also commonly listed on the copyright page.

Copyrighting:

This section is a high level introduction to the important and complex subject of copyrighting in general. This subject must be of great concern to Authors, especially first time Authors as perhaps yourself. It is important that you:

1. Meet copyright laws,
2. Not violate existing copyright laws for material in your book that is copyrighted/owned by others,
3. Secure protection for yourself by using copyright laws to protect the valuable original material in your own book(s).

If your book is massively successful, it will attract the attention of others who might want to share in your royalties by claiming copyright infringement by yourself where you have used material owned by others without proper mention of the source and without permission to publish that material. Similarly if your book is massively successful as we hope, it will be because it contains significant information of interest and value to others, and others might want to use your material disguised as their own, without proper credit (and compensation) due yourself.

from Wikipedia:
"Copyright is a legal concept, enacted by most governments, that grants the creator of an original work exclusive rights to its use and distribution, usually for a limited time, with the intention of enabling the creator of intellectual wealth (e.g. the author of a book) to receive compensation for their work and be able to financially support themselves.

Copyright is a form of intellectual property (as patents, trademarks and trade secrets), applicable to any expressible form of an idea or information that is substantive and discrete.

Copyright may apply to a wide range of creative, intellectual, or artistic forms, or "works". Specifics vary by jurisdiction, but these can include poems, theses, plays and other literary works, motion pictures, choreography, musical compositions, sound recordings, paintings, drawings, sculptures, photographs, computer software, radio and television broadcasts, and industrial designs. Graphic designs and industrial designs may have separate or overlapping laws applied to them in some jurisdictions."

For a complete review of the subject, we suggest you start with:

http://en.wikipedia.org/wiki/Copyright for one of the best reviews at a high level of this complex subject.

In the meantime, be careful to document and credit sources of material in your book to the proper copyright owners. Then everything will go just fine and you should not expect a copyright infringement suit or claimants wanting to "share" any of the huge royalty stream pouring into your bank account each month from your massively successful First Book.

Fleurons:

Fleurons are stylized forms of flowers or leaves used in publishing. Search on *"fleuron images"* on the Internet for public domain fleurons that you might wish to use in your book. Fleurons can also be purchased from publishers and from individuals advertising on the Internet.

Fleuron design used in this book.

Date	1885
Source	*The Raven; with literary and historical commentary*, 1885. Poe. Ingram, et al.,
Author	Printed for George Redway, designer unknown
Permission (Reusing this file)	This media file is in the public domain in the United States. This applies to U.S. works where the copyright has expired, often because its first publication occurred prior to January 1, 1953.

Foreign Language Conversion:
Using statistical machine translation software (SMTS)

As a small time venture capital startup seed and early stage company investor, I have invested in over 30 technology startup companies over the past ten years. One of my early and better investments ROI return on investment wise was Language Weaver. LW, a Los Angeles, California–based company was founded in 2002 by the University of Southern California's Kevin Knight and Daniel Marcu, to commercialize a statistical approach to automatic language translation and natural language processing - now known globally as **statistical machine translation software (SMTS).**

LW was since acquired by SDL, now named SDL Language Weaver.
http://www.sdl.com/products/automated-translation/

SDL Language Weaver's statistically based translation software is an instance of a recent advance in automated translation. While earlier machine translation technology relied on collections of linguistic rules to analyze the source sentence and then map the syntactic and semantic structure into the target language, SDL Language Weaver uses statistical techniques from cryptography. It applies machine learning algorithms that automatically acquire statistical models from existing parallel collections of human translations. These models are more likely to be up to date, appropriate and idiomatic, because they are learned directly from real translations. The software can also be quickly customized to any subject area or style and do a full translation of previously unseen text.

One of the larger proponents of SMT is Google who offers foreign language translation free to customers. A number of companies offer a range of SMT automatic translation services to translate your book's source language into any of over 50 foreign languages.

SMT has not been perfected and is not 100% accurate in instances and between certain pairs of languages. But it does offer an inexpensive and fast alternative at very low cost to translate your book for you into almost any language you wish. SMT learns from itself and perfects conversion accuracy through use. I introduce this subject here in the Appendix because it is an interesting and fairly new technology that is growing in use. If you think you have interest in translating your book into one or more foreign languages, then you need to explore your alternatives in more detail. I have used Google's free translate feature to convert this paragraph (in italics) into ten foreign languages below.

Spanish:

SMT no se ha perfeccionado y no es fiable al 100% en los casos y entre ciertos pares de idiomas. Pero sí ofrece una alternativa económica y rápida para traducir su libro para usted en casi cualquier idioma que desee. SMT aprende de sí misma y perfecciona precisión de la conversión a través del uso. Introduzco este tema aquí en el Apéndice, ya que es una tecnología interesante y bastante nuevo que está creciendo en uso. Si usted piensa que tiene interés en la traducción de su libro en una o más lenguas extranjeras, entonces usted necesita para explorar sus opciones con más detalle. He utilizado característica traducir gratuito de Google para convertir este párrafo en los siguientes idiomas:

French:

SMT n'a pas été mis au point et n'est pas précis à 100% dans les cas et entre certaines paires de langues. Mais il n'offre une alternative peu coûteuse et rapide pour traduire votre livre pour vous dans presque toutes les langues que vous souhaitez. SMT apprend de lui-même et perfectionne la précision de conversion par l'usage. Je présente ce sujet ici dans l'annexe, car il est une technologie intéressante et assez nouvelle qui se développe dans l'utilisation. Si vous pensez que vous avez un intérêt dans la traduction de votre livre dans une ou plusieurs langues étrangères, alors vous devez explorer vos options plus en détail. J'ai utilisé la fonction mains libres traduire de Google pour convertir ce paragraphe dans les langues suivantes:

German:

SMT wurde nicht vollendet und ist nicht 100% genau in Instanzen und zwischen bestimmten Paare von Sprachen. Aber es bietet eine kostengünstige und schnelle Alternative, um Ihr Buch für Sie in nahezu jede gewünschte Sprache zu übersetzen. SMT lernt von selbst und perfektioniert Umwandlungsgenauigkeit durch die Verwendung. Ich stelle dieses Thema hier in der Anlage, weil es ist eine interessante und relativ neue Technologie, die im Einsatz wächst. Wenn Sie denken, dass Sie Interesse an der Übersetzung Ihres Buches in eine oder mehrere Fremdsprachen zu haben, dann müssen Sie Ihre Alternativen näher zu erkunden. Ich habe frei übersetzen Feature von Google verwendet, um dieses Absatzes in den folgenden Sprachen zu konvertieren:

Russian:

SMT пока не совершенна и не на 100% точны в случаях и между определенными парами языков. Но это предлагают недорогой и быстрый альтернативу перевести вашу книгу для вас практически в любом языке, который вы хотите. SMT узнает от себя и совершенствует точность преобразования в процессе использования. Я представляю эту тему здесь в Приложении, потому что это довольно новый и интересная технология, которая растет в использовании. Если вы думаете, у вас есть интерес в переводе вашу книгу в один или несколько иностранных языков, то вам необходимо изучить ваши альтернативы более подробно. Я использовал бесплатный перевести функцию Google, чтобы преобразовать этот пункт на следующие языки:

Japanese:

SMTは完成していない100%の場合において、正確かつ言語の特定のペアの間でされていません。しかし、それはあなたが望むほぼすべての言語にあなたのためのあなたの本を翻訳するために、安価で高速な代替手段を提供していません。
SMTは、自身から学習し、使用して、変換精度を完成。それは、使用中に成長している面白いと比較的新しい技術ですので、私はここに付録のこのテーマをご紹介します。あなたが1つ以上の外国語にあなたの本を翻訳に興味を持っていると思う場合は、より詳細にあなたの選択肢を模索する必要があります。私は以下の言語にこの段落を変換するためにGoogleの無料変換機能を使用していた。

Swedish:

SMT har inte fulländat och är inte 100% korrekt i instanser och mellan vissa par av språk. Men det ger ett billigt och snabbt alternativ till att översätta din bok för dig i nästan alla språk du önskar. SMT lär sig av sig själv och fulländar konvertering noggrannhet genom användning. Jag presentera detta ämne här i tillägget för att det är ett intressant och relativt ny teknik som ökar i användning. Om du tror att du har intresse av att översätta din bok i ett eller flera främmande språk, måste du utforska dina alternativ mer i detalj. Jag har använt Googles kostnadsfria översätta funktion för att omvandla denna punkt till följande språk:

Chinese:

SMT尚未完善，而不是100%准确的情况下和某些对语言之间。但它确实提供了一种廉价和快速的替代翻译你的书你到几乎任何你想要的语言。SMT学会从自身，并通过使用完善的转换精度。我介绍这个主题在这里的附录，因为它是生长在使用一个有趣的和相当新的技术。如果你认为你有在翻译你的书到一个或更多的外国语言的兴趣，那么你需要详细探讨您的选择。我用谷歌的免费翻译功能，本款转换成下列语言：

Greek:

SMT δεν έχει τελειοποιηθεί και δεν είναι 100% ακριβές σε περιπτώσεις και μεταξύ ορισμένων ζεύγη γλωσσών. Αλλά δεν προσφέρουν μια φθηνή και γρήγορη εναλλακτική λύση για να μεταφράσει το βιβλίο σας για σας σε σχεδόν οποιαδήποτε γλώσσα επιθυμείτε. SMT μαθαίνει από την ίδια και τελειοποιεί την ακρίβεια μετατροπής με τη χρήση. Θα εισαγάγει αυτό το θέμα εδώ στο Παράρτημα, διότι είναι μια ενδιαφέρουσα και αρκετά νέα τεχνολογία που αναπτύσσεται κατά τη χρήση. Αν νομίζετε ότι έχετε ενδιαφέρον για την μετάφραση του βιβλίου σας σε μία ή περισσότερες ξένες γλώσσες, τότε θα πρέπει να διερευνήσει εναλλακτικές λύσεις σας με περισσότερες λεπτομέρειες. Έχω χρησιμοποιήσει δωρεάν μεταφράσει χαρακτηριστικό του Google για τη μετατροπή της παρούσας παραγράφου στις ακόλουθες γλώσσες:

Korean:

SMT는 완벽하지 100 % 경우에서 정확한 언어의 특정 쌍 사이에되지 않았습니다. 그러나 당신이 원하는 거의 모든 언어로 당신을 위해 당신의 책을 번역 저렴하고 빠른 대안을 제공 않습니다. SMT는 자체 학습과 사용을 통해 변환 정확도를 완전히한다. 사용 중 성장하고 재미 있고 비교적 새로운 기술이기

때문에 여기에 부록이 주제를 소개합니다. 당신이 하나 이상의 외국어로 당신의 책을 번역에 관심을 가지고 있다고 생각한다면, 당신은 더 많은 세부 사항에 대한 대안을 모색 할 필요가있다. 나는 다음과 같은 언어로이 단락을 변환하는 구글의 무료 번역 기능을 사용하고 있습니다 :

Dutch:
SMT is nog niet geperfectioneerd en is niet 100% accuraat in gevallen en tussen bepaalde paren van talen. Maar het biedt wel een goedkoop en snel alternatief om uw boek voor u vertalen naar vrijwel elke taal die u wilt. SMT leert van zichzelf en perfectioneert nauwkeurigheid conversie door gebruik. Introduceer ik dit onderwerp hier in het aanhangsel, want het is een interessante en vrij nieuwe technologie die groeit in gebruik. Als je denkt dat je interesse hebt in het vertalen van uw boek in een of meer vreemde talen, dan moet u uw alternatieven te onderzoeken in meer detail. Ik heb het gratis Google vertalen functie gebruikt om deze paragraaf te zetten in de volgende talen:

These ten translations combined took me less than two minutes to complete using Google Translate. Over time and through usage, SMT is gaining yearly in translation accuracy. For certain bulk applications it is extremely cost effective as for translating a lengthy romance or adventure novel. However, for certain language pairings between Latin based romance and non romance languages, and for precise scientific translations, the translated document will require additional review and work to assure suitable accuracy for the book purpose.

Try SMT yourself. The technology is amazing and gaining use every day in translating commercial and government documents. After using SMT to translate your book, you can retain a language specialist consultant to complete the translation and verify its accuracy. Search on "eBook translation services" for a list of the many excellent resources (companies and individuals) who will help you to translate your manuscript into any of a number of foreign languages. Costs can run up to $15 per page for a thorough complex translation.

Publishing Across Multiple Distribution Channels:

Once you have published your book on one publisher's platform, you can expand your distribution channels to include other publishers /distributors. Assuming you own the royalty rights to your book, generally you are free to select more than one distributor for your book. And you can even set yourself up as a distributor, buying books direct from your Publisher at the Author discount cost and selling them yourself on the Internet. Although this is possible, it is not recommended. Let the Distributors do their job while you focus on writing books.

1) CreateSpace offers links for distribution channels through Amazon.com/Books and Kindle Direct Publishing.

In addition, it offers expanded distribution for your title. When you enroll your title in the *Bookstores & Online Retailers* or the *Libraries & Academic Institutions* channels, CreateSpace provides your book's information to third-party distributors **Baker & Taylor,** and **Ingram**, respectively. These distributors make your title available to purchase through outside channels. But the decision to buy your book lies solely with individual retailers, libraries, or academic institutions.

---

2) Baker & Taylor:
http://www.btol.com

"Our Business: Baker & Taylor is a leading distributor of books, videos, and music products to libraries, institutions and retailers. We are passionate about books and entertainment products. Many of us have been here for a long time - 20, 30, 40 years. We form deep and lasting bonds with our supplier partners and customers. And we always strive to delight the readers, viewers, and listeners. We have been in business for 181 years and have developed long-term relationships with major book publishers, movie studios and music labels. We have more than 36,000 customers in more than 120 countries.

We ship more than 1 million unique products (SKUs) annually. We also maintain one of the largest in-stock inventories of books, videos and music in the U.S. - about 385,000 titles in inventory and more than 1.5 million titles available for order. We have substantially increased our book inventory with our new Print on Demand Program, allowing customers to access the titles they need when they need them. Baker & Taylor also provides books and entertainment products to warehouse clubs and Internet retailers and publishes several successful lines of books, including the best-selling Uncle John's Bathroom Reader series.

Baker & Taylor is also committed to being an industry leader in digital media delivery. Through best-of-breed technologies, Baker & Taylor offers its publishers and customers bundled physical and digital media distribution services. We empower publishers to manage content distribution in multiple formats, to numerous digital devices and merchandising channels worldwide. We supply customers both the physical books and digital content they want, from one trusted source. As the digital future takes shape, Baker & Taylor is delivering success for suppliers and customers.

Want to know more about Baker & Taylor? Just click www.btol.com to find out more about our history, our senior management team, our locations, a career with Baker & Taylor, or recent news."

3) Ingram:

www.ingramcontent.com/pages/ingram-publisher-services.aspx

"Services for Authors and small Publishers:

We work with over 28,000 small and independent publishers around the world, offering a simplified path into the world's largest print and electronic content distribution network.

If you've written a book--but it isn't quite "done" yet--Ingram has built relationships with partners that offer specialized services to help, such as: design, developing print-ready and e-ready files, editorial, publicity and marketing , or even comprehensive author services.

Ready for distribution? If your books are already on the market--or you have all the pieces of a finished book in place--you may be ready to begin a direct relationship with Ingram.

Explore the links below to learn more about Ingram global publisher services:

- •Worldwide Content (Print & Electronic) Distribution
- •Inventory Management
- •Printing Services

- E-book Services
- E-commerce Services"

In addition to the CreateSpace/Amazon.com/Books distributors described herein as the method we chose to publish our book initially, and in addition to working with Ingram or Baker and Taylor, we can also pursue working directly with other distributor channels. Here are three more of the most popular distributors. We have included reprints of the introduction information from each of the vendor websites.

- Google Books
- Barnes & Noble
- Apple iBooks Store

---

4) Google Books:

https://support.google.com/books/partner

"An introduction to the Google Books Partner Program: There are two components to the Google Books Partner Program:

1) The Preview Program is a free marketing program that enables publishers and authors to promote their books online, through Google Books. By submitting a digital or physical copy of your book so it can be previewed online, you'll make it discoverable to Google users from around the world.

When a reader finds your book on Google Books, they'll see a limited preview of your book, as well as a series of links to purchase your title at major online retailers. You can also add a custom link to the book's listing on your own website.

2) Additionally, partners in some countries can sell digital editions of their books on Google Play, earning revenue whenever users purchase their eBooks. Books must be made previewable on Google Books in order to be sold on Google Play.

How Google Books works: We scan the full text of your book, to make each word of your title a possible result for a search on Google Books. This means that if the word "guitar" appears in a page of your book, it would appear as a result for a user searching the word [guitar]. However, even though we index all pages of your title, you can control the percentage of your book that a user will be able to browse.

We've also integrated the Google Books index with the index of Google Web Search, so our users from all around the world will be able to discover your books.

How previews on Google Books work: This video explains how to browse books on Google Books and the different preview settings depending on the type of content source.

Your content is protected: We host all book content on our secure servers. We disable the print, cut, copy, and save functionality on all preview pages displaying book content, in order to protect your material.

Google also protects your content by limiting the number of pages that are shown to users. You can choose to make from 20% to 100% of your book's content browsable. Partners who wish can also choose to make a PDF of their book available to users for download.

If you sell books on Google Play, you can choose to apply DRM (Digital Rights Management) to your eBooks. You will retain your copyright. Google does not assume any copyright to your material.

Your benefits: On the preview page for your book, we display a set of links to buy the book at the websites of major retailers, as well as to a site of your choice. These links are not paid for by the sites featured, and clicking on a link to purchase your book at an online retailer won't generate any revenue directly.

The exception is if you also make the book available for sale on Google Play. Learn more about selling your books through Google.

How to submit your book: We offer you the ability to send us a file in PDF or ePub format, or a physical copy of your title. If you send us a hard copy, we use proprietary scanning technology to prepare your book for display on Google Books. However, our scanning process requires that your books be dismantled -- as a result, we're unable to return physical books to you.

If you're interested in joining the Google Books Partner Program, sign up now. We look forward to welcoming you as a partner."

---

5) Barnes & Noble:

www.barnesandnobleinc.com/for_authors/for_authors.html

"A Vast Selection Means More Opportunities for Your Book.
Our livelihood depends on the authors whose works line our shelves. At Barnes & Noble, we believe the best way for us to serve our authors is to make sure we can tell our customers, "Yes, we can get that book for you."

That's why we stock as wide a selection as possible in our stores – over 100,000 unique book titles per store. And, **we stock over 1 million unique titles in our warehouse** – that's more than any of our competitors or even the largest book wholesalers. This inventory is connected to the customer service stations in our stores in "real-time," so customers can walk into our stores at any time and access books that are not on our shelves.

Because no two Barnes & Noble stores are alike, we also tailor our selection to each store. Our store managers play a central role in deciding what titles are stocked in their stores, and they have the additional authority and responsibility to reorder books to fill local demand.

Customers can walk into our stores at any time looking for titles that are not on our shelves. These requests are usually random and unpredictable: they could be generated by a local book group, a report on the radio, or a review in a specialty magazine. Bookstores used to acquire these titles by placing special orders with publishers. This often resulted in low fill rates (few publishers have "real-time" inventory) and long delivery times -- as much as 4-6 weeks.

We decided that the best way for us to say "yes" more times to our customers was to stock more titles on the shelves of our warehouse. This inventory is connected to the customer service stations in our stores in "real-time," and means we can say "yes" across titles from 40,000 unique publisher imprints, including small presses, university presses and independently published books.

Our largest store of all is our Web site. Our extensive warehouse stock enables Barnes & Noble.com to ship more titles faster than any online bookseller. In addition to our great service, our Web site offers these features:
Comprehensive bibliographic information
- Cover scans – our research has shown that a book without a cover scan has less chance to sell
- Publisher synopsis, editorial reviews and customer reviews
- Table of contents
- Reading group guides

Additionally, Barnes & Noble.com has invested in advanced search and browse technologies that enable our customers to find the books they want or might be interested in:

- Search engine, BookBrowser, and Book recommendations

For Vendors and Publishers:
www.barnesandnobleinc.com/for_publishers/for_publishers.html

All suppliers, manufacturers and other vendors (collectively, "Vendors") of Barnes & Noble and its subsidiaries and affiliates must comply with the Barnes & Noble Vendor Requirements.

We stock over 100,000 unique book titles in our stores and over 1 million unique titles in our warehouse – more than any of our competitors or even the largest book wholesalers. Our vast inventory contains over 50,000 publisher imprints, including small presses, university presses and independently published books.

The sheer volume of books we carry demonstrates our commitment to a wide variety of publishers. Every year we review more than 100,000 submissions from both large and small publishers from diverse backgrounds. Our buyers review publishers' catalogues, marketing materials and galleys or sample copies to help make their decisions. Most of these books are added to our book database and a small order is placed for our warehouse. This makes the title available for sale on our website and for order through our stores. If you would like our buyers to consider your title, please see How to Submit a Book.

To ensure that our vendors get their books and other products on sale in our stores and online as quickly as possible, we provide Vendor Policies and Guidelines developed according to voluntary industry standards prepared by the Book Industry Study Group (BISG).

The Discover Great New Writers Program highlights the best new and undiscovered contemporary writers, and since its inception in 1990, has introduced readers to Neil Gaiman, Elizabeth Gilbert, Khaled Hosseini, Kazuo Ishiguro, Cormac McCarthy, Jodi Picoult, and Michael Pollan, among others.

Publishers recommend writers who are making a strong literary debut, and a small group of Barnes & Noble bookseller volunteers convenes year-round to review submissions to the program and to choose a selection of new books per season for special promotion.

Annually, we recognize two of our exceptional writers with the Discover Great New Writers Award (one each for Fiction and Non-Fiction)."

---

6) Apple iBooks Store:
http://www.apple.com/ibooks-author

"You can submit your book for publication on the iBooks Store, or export it in a variety of formats and distribute it yourself. Before you can publish to the iBooks Store, you need to do the following:

Get an Apple ID (a user name you can use to shop the iTunes Store, log in to iCloud, and more). If you don't have an Apple ID or aren't sure if you have one, go to the My Apple ID website.

Sign up for a Free or Paid Books Account. You can sign up during the publishing process (after you click Publish). Signing up for an account is free. Free Books Account: If you are going to offer only books for free, create a Free Books Account. If you create a Free Books Account and decide to sell books, you need to create a Paid Books Account.

Paid Books Account: To sell books on the iBooks Store, you need a Paid Books Account (you can still offer books for free if you like). With a Paid Books Account, you need to provide banking and tax information so that you can receive payments for the books you sell on the iBooks Store. After you create your Paid Books Account, sign in and activate your contract.

Download iTunes Producer, the application you use to deliver your book to the iBooks Store. You can download iTunes Producer for free as part of the publishing process.

Create a sample book (required with a Paid Books Account) for customers to view for free before deciding to purchase your book. During the publishing process, iBooks Author can create a sample based on one of your book's chapters. Or, you can create a sample manually. Books submitted to the iBooks Store using a Paid Books Account can be protected by Apple's proprietary FairPlay DRM (digital rights management) system, which helps prevent unauthorized duplication of your book."

Maximizing Your Royalties:

You are self-publishing your book as part of your permanent legacy to the world and to make a significant contribution to the collective storehouse of information that powers the world and its people. You are not publishing primarily to make money.

However, making a lot of money from your book is a very worthy secondary objective and outcome because it means that you have produced a very valuable product that people are willing to purchase.

Setting the initial price is tricky because you have no idea of the price/demand curve. But the risk is lowered considerably because you retain the ability to adjust the price of your book over time. This flexibility allows you to encourage initial popularity of your book by offering it at a lower price, and then once you are in production for awhile and book sales are proceeding at the original price you set for your book, you can at any time in the future increase the price of the book to increase your royalty margin. The cost to the Buyer will include shipping and handling (typically around $3.60), plus sales tax (est. $1.60), so the total cost without a distribution channel discount for this $18.00 book would be closer to $23.00.

Similarly if initial sales do not meet your expectation, you can lower the price in the future to increase sales. Most online self-publishing services described in this book have sophisticated computer software that allows you to easily adjust your book price up and down at any time and by any amount. With print on demand, there are no warehousing costs to advance print and store your book.

For this book which is published by CreateSpace and distributed initially through Amazon.com and Kindle Direct Publishing, changes to the list price will be updated on Createspace and KDP immediately, on Amazon.com/Books within three to five business days, and take up to six weeks to fully propagate through outside Expanded Distribution channels.

This is a good marketing strategy for your book. Just keep in mind that the price may not go lower than the minimum list price that has been set for you to cover the base cost to produce your book. Welcome to the big brave new world of Self-publishing.

World Knowledge Growth Trends driving Self-Publishing futures:

I am writing this book, working in my office/library, surrounded by old friends, the hundreds of books I have purchased over the years, written by Authors (producers) who have reached out to me and said *"Jon, how may I help you understand?"* Each book helped me at the time to better understand what was going on in my life and in the world around me. Each book is marked up, page corners turned down, key sentences underlined, and yellow highlighter marks key paragraphs. I can easily reach up and quickly scan each book, whenever need or interest arise, and re-examine the key subjects of the book. I am on my tenth read of *Generations* now to include a quote for this book. Each one of these books "saved my life" in one fashion or another as I resonated to the truths being revealed within.

Where I have a history of direct personal experience or interaction with Authors including David Boren, William Nordhaus, Jean Shinoda Bolen, Robert Shiller, Stephen Covey, Judith Wallerstein, Bud Conrad, Leonard Schlain and John Lahr, their books are like having each one of them sitting next to me again in my office in my old leather easy chair, discussing one on one subjects of mutual import and gaining the emotional intimacy that is so hard (for men in particular) to achieve physically one on one as each Author reveals his or her mind, heart, soul and concerns to me and to the world through his or her writing. Marjorie Dunstan would not like this previous sentence. (*"Too long, punctuate!"* she would have said.). Sorry Ms. Dunstan, I was on a roll and had to get the ideas out. I retain it only to show my former style.

A subject area for an entire separate book is the challenge of how can an Author's information that is self-published be indexed into useful knowledge. The challenge is introduced here within the specific subject area of self-publishing. Answering that challenge requires a serious discussion of how to "index" this ever growing base of information into knowledge that is findable and sharable for the benefit of others.

Turning **information** (data) into **knowledge** (indexed data blended and tempered with experience) is a real challenge. It involves the principle of synergy where people, ideas and information come together to create knowledge that is beneficial to individuals and the society of nations. Personal computing, the Internet, and powerful linking technologies are the tools we will use most to meet the challenge of converting information into knowledge through indexing. IBM had an old advertising slogan mantra from the 1970s:

*"**Not just data, Reality!**"*   Today that would be:

*"**Not just information, Knowledge**!"*

But the point remains the same, use the power of computing technology to convert information (out of context and meaningless on its own) into knowledge of use to humankind.

Jon's Bookshelf:

50 random selections from my bookshelf include:

The Seasons of a Man's Life   by Daniel Levinson

The Seven Principles for Making Marriage Work   J. Gottman & N. Silver

The Alphabet versus the Goddess   by Leonard Shlain

The Enneagram   by Helen Palmer

When Bad Things Happen to Good People   by Harold Kushner

The Healing Heart   by Norman Cousins

Healthy Pleasures   by Robert Ornstein

Woman - An Intimate Geography   by Natalie Angier

Cycles of Power   by Pamela Levin

What Color is Your Parachute?   by Richard Bolles

The Astrology Sun Signs   (for yourself and a significant other)

MegaTrends 2000   by John Naisbitt

Habits of the Heart   by Robert Bellah

Fire in the Belly   by Sam Keen

Principle Centered Leadership   by Stephen Covey

Goddesses in Every Woman   by Jean Shinoda Bolen

Emotional Intelligence   by Daniel P. Goleman

You Just Don't Understand   by Barbara Tannen

The Road Less Traveled   by M. Scott Peck

What Your Mother Couldn't Tell You & Your Father Didn't Know J. Gray

A Course in Miracles

The Good Marriage   by Judith Wallerstein

Modern Man in Search of a Soul   by C.G. Jung

How We Die   by Sherwin Nuland

Stewardship   by Peter Block

The Fifth Discipline   by Peter Senge

The Seven Habits of Highly Effective People   by Stephen Covey

All I Really Need to Know I Learned in Kindergarten   by R. Fulgham

Care of the Soul   by M. Thomas Moore

Hot, Flat and Crowded   by Thomas Friedman

Miss Manners' Guide to Excruciatingly Correct Behavior   Judith Martin
The Deming Management Method   W. Edwards Deming & M. Walton
Why Zebras Don't Get Ulcers   by Robert Sapolsky
The Great Crash Ahead   by Harry L. Dent
Collapse   by Jared Diamond
The Color of Oil   by Michael Economides and Ronald Oligney
The Post American World   by Fareed Zakaria
Jesus- CEO   by Laurie Beth Jones
The Passion of the Western Mind   by Richard Tarnas
Healthy Pleasures   by Robert Ornstein and David Sobel
The New Joy of Sex   by Alex Comfort
The Coming Global Boom   by Charles Morris
Solitude   by Anthony Storr
Smithsonian Ocean – Our Water Our World
Cosmos   by Carl Sagan
The Path to Love   by Deepak Chopra
The Origin of Species   by Charles Darwin

And now one more just added to my still growing book collection...
Self-Publish Your Own Book – a (simple) Guide - Yale 1963 Authors
by Jon H. Larson

As I look over the books on my shelf today, here are three of them with very special meaning to me.

"*A Letter to America*" by classmate David Boren, boldly asks the question of how long the United States, with only six percent of the world's population, can remain a global superpower. He explains with unsparing clarity why the country is at a crossroads and why decisive action is urgently needed. He draws on his experiences as the longest-serving chair of the U.S. Senate's Intelligence Committee, as governor of Oklahoma, and now as president of the University of Oklahoma.

The Climate Casino: Risk, Uncertainty, and Economics for a Warming World by William Nordhaus. William is a fellow Yale classmate, a former member of the President's Council of Economic Advisors, is currently a Yale economics professor, and was recently appointed chairman of the Federal Reserve of Boston. In our college days we spent a Christmas vacation together as guests of my Aunt Pokey and Uncle Ed Porter in Wilmington, Delaware where we attended a fun round of coming out parties over the holidays. Bill and our mutual roommate Randy Ryan taught this old surfer from Hawaii how to snow ski in Vermont our Freshman year in 1959. He explains how climate change is profoundly altering our world in ways that pose major risks to human societies and natural systems. We have entered the Climate Casino and are rolling the global-warming dice he warns. But there is still time to turn around and walk back out of the casino, and in this essential book he explains how. Bringing together all the important issues surrounding the climate debate, he describes the science, economics, and politics involved—and the steps necessary to reduce the perils of global warming.

Generations: The History of America's Future, 1584 to 2069 by Neil Howe and William Strauss. Written in 1991 and first read by me in 1992, it predicts a Crisis Era in our country from approximately 2014 to 2036 repeating a recurring theme of four 22 year general cycles within a repeating overall 88 year cycle of eras they have named;

1) Awakening, 2) Inner Driven, 3) Crisis, and 4) Outer Driven.

We are soon to repeat the previous 88 year cycle Crisis Eras of intense societal stress and change that will match in intensity the Revolutionary War (1770's), the Civil War (1840's), and the Great Depression (1930's) as we now approach the next Crisis Era which promises to be every much as gripping and traumatic as the previous three Crisis Eras experienced in our collective history. The coming Crisis Era is described as follows;

.... _"From unsustainable entitlements to insufficient investment, from decaying infrastructure to an American economy controlled by foreign creditors, from Third World revolution to nuclear proliferations, from depleted fossil fuels to a poisoned atmosphere –"- ,_

all will come to a point and must be dealt with in this coming 22 year Crisis Era. The book goes on to describe alternative outcomes for us based on the leadership that emerges from the Boomer generation that leads us; --

"Let us hope that old Boomers will look within themselves and find something richer than apocalypse. If they see and assert themselves as beacons of civilization, younger Americans may well look up to them as G.I.'s did to the great Missionary leaders, as elders wise beyond the comprehension of youth. If the Gray Champions among them can seize *this historic opportunity, they can guide a unified national community through the gates of history to a better world beyond. "* ….

Writing further, *"No one can foretell the specific emergency that will confront America during what we call the 'Crisis of 2020' – nor of course, the exact year in which this crisis will find its epicenter. What we do claim our cycle can predict is that during the late 2010's and the early 2020's, American generations will pass deep into a 'Crisis Era' constellation and mood, and that, as a consequence, the nation's public life will undergo a swift and possibly revolutionary transformation."*

Interested? For 530 more pages of supporting detail, buy the book and read it as it describes "the history of our future."

The Mind/Imagination Connection:

Supplementing my book shelf is Karen's own bookshelf in her sewing room with over 1,000 books purchased over the years, mostly softcover and fiction oriented. Karen reads fiction plus books on sewing and cook books. I read non-fiction; self-help, business and technology trends, history trends, and spiritual enlightenment. Plus we have subscribed over the years to the Great Books series and have gold trimmed leather bound books of the Great Works on shelves in our family room and bedroom. Between us we have it all covered.

In addition we share numerous books we download and store on Karen's Kindle including *Unbroken: A World War II Story of Survival, Resilience, and Redemption* by Laura Hillenbrand. Assisting Karen recently to archive off many of the books stored in her Kindle, I came across *Unbroken* again. In this fascinating story of WWII being made into a movie by Angelina Jolie, I read about the airfield at Kahuku on the north shore of Oahu, Hawaii during WWII where Army Air Force bombardier Louie Zamperini and his 372nd B-24 Liberator squadron practiced bombing runs, planning and preparing and training for the eventual retaking of the Pacific theater.

I myself do not remember much of the war, having spent the day of the December 7th bombing of Pearl Harbor, just six days old, resting comfortably with my Mother after our child birthing ordeal in Kapiolani Maternity Hospital. Back in those days mothers received 10-14 days rest and recuperation in the hospital after childbirth. Today mothers get two days if lucky but are usually up and out within a day with delivery hospitals operating more like a MacDonald's fast food drive through. My mother said she actually looked forward to childbirth in those days because she got two weeks in the hospital alone being attended to, while Dad and the other children somehow managed at home. A mini-vacation from motherly duties.

I spent wonderful moments in my youth in the 1950's within five miles of that same Kahuku airfield, long since abandoned by the military, now with the surrounding land converted to fresh water shrimp farming and a wind mill electricity generation farm built by Dudley Pratt as president of Hawaiian Electric. His father Dudley senior encouraged me to attend Yale after Punahou for which I will always be grateful. HECO employed my father and was my family's bread and butter for 40 years. The smartly positioned wind farm takes advantage of the non-stop 24x7 gentle trade winds that blow from the north, touch down at HECO's wind mill farm on their route up and over the Koolau Mountain range to the south, and then over the Island of Oahu to cool downtown Honolulu before they return to the sea from whence they came.

I recall my best high school friend Jimbo Haley and I taking our old jalopies, his a '48 Dodge, and mine a '39 Chevy, out onto the asphalt of the airstrip for organized drag races. And playing golf with my father at the Kahuku golf course maintained by the long defunct Kahuku Sugar Plantation. In late afternoons, we would often have the entire course to ourselves, the most lovely little nine hole golf course in the world, right along the lava rocks and sands and blue Pacific ocean of the Oahu north shore. And near all of the beaches where I surfed in the 1950's including Haleiwa, Pupukea, Kawailoa, Sunset Beach and Waimea Bay. We surfed all day long, and virtually alone by today's crowded standards. We dove for lobsters and sea shells in Kawela Bay and at Shark's Cove, and we body surfed at Pounders in Haena. All just 15 years after Louie Zamperini and his B-24 squadron were flying practice runs out of Kahuku airfield for deadly serious and dangerous missions in a full scale war in the Pacific Theater yet to be decided.

I am reminded by this book once again of the beauty and richness of the written word, and how we are rewarded time and time again by someone taking the time to publish an interesting story. And how I was completely unaware of the important history of that old Kahuku airfield until I read the book. And how compared to the trials and tribulations of Zamperini mistreated as a prisoner of war, I can electronically download his story over a wireless connection from my comfortable easy chair with the touch of a finger and effortlessly flip through the pages of his life story. **The mind/imagination connection is an awesome and powerful synergy and one of the great joys in life as Authors lead us on amazing adventures with the carefully crafted words in their books.** They are tour guides, taking the rest of us along on their own journeys of discovery.

The Knowledge based economy:

We converted from an agricultural based economy to a manufacturing based economy, and now are rapidly converting to an information economy where managing, indexing, processing and selling information continue at an accelerating rate. We went from producing food, to producing hard goods, to producing information.

We understand that the rate of production of information and indexing it into useful knowledge is accelerating with technology advances of computers, software, and the Internet, supported by the legions of people documenting their findings in published books, both self-published and the good old fashioned way with an agent and a publisher. Google, Bing, Yahoo, Ask, About and over 200 other search engines listed on *http://www.thesearchenginelist.com/* provide us rapid indexed access to the growing volume of data stored in the Internet "cloud". Organizations as Wikipedia are making useful information available to us at no cost, supported by legions of volunteers who as self-appointed SME's, Subject Matter Experts, guard, maintain, index and enhance key information.

Robert J. Shiller is a 2013 Nobel laureate in economics, a Professor of Economics at Yale University, and the co-creator of the Case-Shiller Index of US house prices. He was the author of *Irrational Exuberance* in 2000 which correctly predicted the dot.com bubble collapse, the second edition of which predicted the then coming collapse of the real-estate bubble, and most recently, *Finance and the Good Society.*

As early as 2004, Shiller projected changes in the global financial system and the electronic money revolution regarding conversion to a fully electronic banking system worldwide; *"The economic revolution (of electronic banking) may be as profound as that wrought by our ancient ancestors' invention of coins."*

He also wrote *".... the magnitude of transaction costs and contracting costs ultimately determine much of an economy's structure. As **new forms of money** reduce these costs, the richness and complexity of our economy will be increased. Lower transaction costs* *mean that exchange can be dramatically more fine-grained. With the latest forms of **electronic money we can sell millions of little things, to millions of different people, all over the world.** Nowhere is this more important than **in the realm of ideas.**"* The realm of ideas includes the self-publishing industry where I can produce this book and offer it for sale on a global basis, without exchanging one single physical dollar of currency.

The hardcover *Irrational Exuberance* sitting on my shelf at home is personally signed with the inscription *"Glad to help out. Congratulations on your market timing. Best Wishes, Robert J. Shiller."* It was signed at a presentation I attended at his Yale School of Management. I purchased his book for $26.00 in May of 2000 when the NASDAQ Composite hit 4,800 and projections were it would break 5,000 by summer. I took it along and read his book on an Alaska cruise ship. Within a week of returning home to San Francisco I had converted 100% of our dot.com tech portfolio back into cash, a month before the NASDAQ commenced its sickening 75% drop to 1,200 within two years (it has since recovered slowly back to 4,075 today). That $26.00 book and the two hours taken from my vacation time to read it saved me over $300,000 in stock losses. It is clearly the best investment I will ever make, other than marrying Karen 50 years ago of course. That investment was and will always be, "priceless."

It is my fondest hope that the less than $20.00 you spent to acquire this book will yield you a similar multiple return on investment by using the information herein to enable you to succeed in a new endeavor that benefits others (and yourself).

Self-publishing and selling books, even in small quantities including units of one, can be profitable to the Author thanks to the trends towards a knowledge based economy, electronic book distribution, and electronic banking. Thanks to electronic banking, you have a global market for your self-published book with electronic payment into your bank account without exchange and handling of small amounts of physical cash per transaction. We take electronic banking for granted. Today 93% of the world's currency exists in electronic form only, and projections are that the conversion to a 100% electronic form of currency (doing away with the physical greenback, coins and even paper checks), will be accomplished this year (see trends at the end of this Appendix). Media coverage has failed to look far enough into the future and to comprehend the full extent of the changes that will be wrought by new forms of electronic money as people and businesses invent new ways of doing business. Electronic money, as it develops, will eventually transform the world economy.

A newsletter I get monthly predicts the beginning of the end of the U.S. greenback dollar this year as the U.S. initiates a final thrust to complete the conversion to the all electronic money system, eliminating physical money (cash, coins and checks). One projection tells us this could happen as early as this year at a future meeting of the Federal Reserve under its new Chairman Janet Yellen where there will be a permanent affirmation to low (no) interest and pumping electronic funds into the banking system as the world accelerates to an all electronic banking system. The newsletter says this is not some doomsday scenario. The event we are about to experience could bring a short term crisis but also historic opportunity. It will transform almost every industry, economy and society. It could even spawn new branches of human endeavor that will lead us out of the current malaise. My immediate thought is that one outcome will be the reduction of street crime related to drugs when a cashless system forces all transactions to occur via traceable bank debit cards.

Shiller writes further..."*Two benefits of electronic money stand out and will likely contribute to its growth. Most important, it will have profound intellectual benefits by creating incentives for the **active pursuit of ideas**. Second, electronic money will advance globalization, expanding the scope and versatility of the Internet and making it easier for people to interact constructively with others around the world. Taken together, these two benefits will enable millions of minds to work together far more effectively than ever before.*"

Quoting from an April, 2014 business newsletter to which I subscribe;

"Using its **FedWire** network, the Federal Reserve can now transmit money between every major financial institution in the world. That includes thousands of banks such as First National American Bank in East Lansing, Michigan and Bank of America San Francisco. They also include Wall Street firms such as Morgan Stanley, HSBC America, J.P. Morgan Chase, Citibank and Deutsche Bank. FedWire capillaries pump money into the world's tiniest banks, too, such as the Safeway Employees Credit Union of Los Angeles and the Tempe Schools Credit Union. Every single major financial institution on earth now transmits commerce via FedWire. Ginnie Mae ... Freddie Mac ... Fannie Mae ... the U.S. Treasury ... the Asian Development Bank ... the list goes on. FedWire also serves as the hub for the world's electronic central-banking system today. You have the People's Bank of China ... the European Central Bank ... the Bank of Japan ... the Central Bank of Brazil. .. the Saudi Arabian Monetary Agency ... the Swiss National Bank. .. the Bank of Central African States ... all connecting through this single computer network. In the background of our financial system, FedWire now processes more than 127,022,420 transactions per year. The average value of these transactions is $5.23 million dollars. Last year alone, FedWire facilitated more than $662.8 trillion in new commerce. And we expect that number to increase in 2014 ... dramatically ...."

Sitting next to *Irrational Exuberance* on my bookshelf is Harry Dent's new book *The Great Crash Ahead.* *Let's* hope that Dent's prediction of the return of the boom/bust economic cycle with massive deflation and unprecedented economic upheaval ahead does not play itself out in the coming 22 year Crisis Era now on our doorstep according to *Generations*. A successful conversion to an all electronic money system which accelerates the global economy and our standard of living is certainly preferable. Other "gold bugs" predict the current Federal Reserve "fiat money" massive debt fueled bubble will eventually collapse, ending in elimination of the Federal Reserve and issuance of U.S. Treasury notes to replace the Federal Reserve fiat greenback dollars with a pre-1971 gold backed dollar. Others predict the eventual end of the U.S. dollar as the sole world's reserve currency which would cause massive disruptions to our standard of living and our way of life as we know it. We have an exciting future in store for us. And many opportunities for self-publishers to weigh in on these matters. Now back to the main subject of this book.

Knowledge defined:

http://www.merriam-webster.com/dictionary/knowledge
knowl·edge   *noun* \'nä-lij\
: information, understanding, or skill from experience or education
: awareness of something : the state of being aware of something
Full Definition of KNOWLEDGE:
2a (1) : the fact or condition of knowing something with familiarity gained through experience or association
4a : the sum of what is known : the body of truth, information, and principles acquired by humankind

The Knowledge Doubling Curve:

Since its creation in 1989, the growth of the WWW - World Wide Web has been so fast that it is virtually impossible to get anyone to agree on a set of statistics describing accurately the number of servers, URL web site addresses, the number of HTML pages, and the total amount of information stored in the web. Figures using billions and trillions are used casually, and the mind cannot comprehend its size and growth. In his 1982 book *Critical Path*, futurist and inventor R. Buckminster Fuller estimated that if we took all the knowledge that mankind had accumulated and transmitted by the Year One CE as equal to one unit of information, it probably took about 1,500 years or until the sixteenth century for that amount of knowledge to double. The next doubling of knowledge from two to four 'knowledge units' took only 250 years, until about 1750 CE. By 1900, one hundred and fifty years later, knowledge had doubled again to 8 units. Fuller created the *"Knowledge Doubling Curve"* to describe the growth in information, and he did this seven years before the WWW was imagined, much less created. When plotted on a graph *"The Knowledge Doubling Curve"* looks like a hockey stick curve (see diagram) but the curve is not that smooth. Certain key events have been like thresholds. The invention of writing, then of printing (first in China, then later in Europe) were significant thresholds. But the invention of the World Wide Web allowed for exponential increase in the speed of knowledge doubling.

By the end of World War II knowledge was doubling every 25 years. Different types of knowledge have different rates of growth. Nanotechnology knowledge is doubling every two years and clinical knowledge every 18 months. But on average human knowledge now is doubling every 13 months. According to one futuristic projection from IBM, the eventual build out of the "internet of things" could lead to the doubling of knowledge every 12 hours.

When I graduated from college in 1963, there was no World Wide Web, no PC or laptop computers, no email, no fax machines, no voice mail, no DVD, no satellite TV, no mobile phones, no PDA's (Ipads, IPods, Nooks, Mac Air's nor Nooks), no digital cameras, no blogs and no Wikipedia. Today the growth rate of the Internet is accelerating at such a degree that stating the numbers and the growth are almost meaningless because any numbers we project here today will most likely be exceeded.

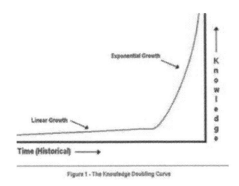

Human Brain Indexing Will Consume Several Billion Petabytes

In a lecture at Harvard University neuroscientist Jeff Lichtman, who is attempting to map the human brain, has calculated that several billion petabytes of data storage would be needed to index the entire human brain. The Internet is currently estimated to be 5 million terabytes (TB) of which Google has indexed roughly 200 TB or just .004% of its total size. The numbers involved are astounding, especially when considering the size of the human brain and the number of neurons it contains.

Linear to Exponential Growth of Human Knowledge

A transition from the linear growth of human knowledge to the exponential growth of human knowledge has taken place. According to researchers, dealing with this information will necessitate the development of vastly more complex software, indexing for shareability, and artificial intelligence.

Author Clem Chambers, in a Forbes article on Amazon's "Mechanical Turk" believes leading edge computer technology will be combined with artificial intelligence allowing collective problem-solving on a larger scale and the creation of even vaster amounts of data.

The following diagram purports to show information growth in the world today. This book you are reading is 5mb (5 million characters) when stored on a computer. 200 of these books is 1gb. 1,000 gb is 1 terabyte. 1,000 terabytes is one petabyte. And 1,000 petabytes is 1 exabyte. 1 exabyte is 2/3rds of the world's annual production of information. So this book represents the combined length of 5 tiny ants compared to the total yearly growth of our information base which is comparatively 1.5 x the diameter of the sun.

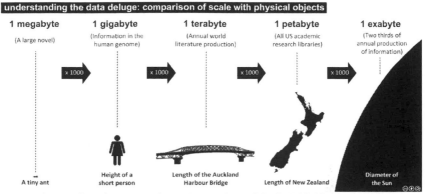

Understanding the Data Deluge: Comparison of Scale With Physical Objects (Infographic created by Julian Carver of Seradigm http://www.seradigm.co.nz)

How has change increased? Let us look at two examples from history: the speed of transportation and the acceleration of knowledge. Around 6,000 BC the camel caravan was the fastest form of transportation at about eight miles an hour. In the late eighteenth century (1785) the stagecoach was able to cover about ten miles an hour. It took about 8,000 years to increase the average group speed by two miles an hour. In 1825 the steam engine was invented and within a decade locomotives could carry people at a speed of thirteen miles an hour. In less than fifty years the average rate of speed had increased more than in the previous 8,000 years. Within the next one hundred years airplanes were going 100 miles an hour and by 1960 missiles were traveling at over 1,800 mph. This rapid acceleration in the speed of travel has transformed our planet and brought tremendous change in its wake.

Once change begins, it can gather momentum like a snowball rolling down hill. Soon we are buried in the avalanche of change that had a small beginning.

No wonder we have a hard time keeping up with the latest data. Trying to stay current with the knowledge base in just a limited area of interest is impossible. When you move out of this familiar area, sifting through the maze of information is mind boggling. We are seeing more and more specialization as people try to control and limit the size of the information pool with which they must be familiar.

Expanding knowledge exponentially through linkages:

Focusing on the particular subject of self-publishing, I have tried to make this book a "one stop shop" that links the reader to the broad spectrum of companies and resources in the industry. I have included over 80 direct Internet URL "links" to other web sites containing additional detailed information. In this way I have attempted to magnify the usefulness of this book. Including links to other information sources increases the synergy by combining my own findings with those of others into an integrated neural network where the reader is encouraged to branch out to other sources when needed for more information stored elsewhere on any particular subject.

This is how we create intelligence and knowledge from the massive and growing amount of information we produce. I have put my effort into organizing this book and presenting the large number of additional resources out there to place the reader into the system of self-publishing support. By trying to be a single source starting point and reference source, I am helping the reader to better understand this industry within which he or she is going to publish his or her first book. The reader can leave this book at any point and branch out to any of the recommended outside sources, and hopefully return back here, or not.

This is one writing technique that self-publishers can implement in their book to integrate themselves into the larger whole. It is relatively easy to present information cut and pasted from other sources. It is a lot more difficult and very hard work to present this information in an organized fashion that guides the reader through the entire system from start to end, while freeing the reader to traverse through many paths to get there.

We cannot assume that the rapid growth in human knowledge is happening all around us, naturally and painlessly. In fact human knowledge about a particular subject can increase fast or faster, but it is almost always as a result of putting together money, institutional resources, and interested and bright people to do the research. It helps to have an urgent public need or potential private gain as a carrot. But where these inputs are not provided, human knowledge about a subject grows at a much slower rate.

It is said that possibly up to half of the knowledge we accepted 50 years ago is outdated or flat out wrong today. Yesterday's "truth and knowledge" sometimes become today's myths and undoings.

As shown in patents and academic publications, knowledge doubles at different rates for different sectors, ranging from two years for nanotechnology to 21 years for other sectors. The term *Singularity* was popularized more than a decade ago by the mathematician, computer scientist, and science fiction novelist Vernor Vinge, who borrowed the term from mathematics and astrophysics. It refers to the future point at which technological change, propelled by the explosive growth of artificial intelligence, will accelerate past the point of current human comprehension. So how do we keep our sanity?

The Emerging world wide web of the Spirit:

United Religions Initiative:

World Interfaith Harmony Week declared by the UN each year reminds me when in 1992 I visited William Swing, the Bishop of the Episcopal Diocese of California in his office at Grace Cathedral. I called and asked to discuss an idea, using the 50th anniversary of the United Nations Charter signing in SF in June of 1945 as an opportunity to create a United Religions interfaith organization modeled after the UN, but serving the mutual needs of the world's major faith traditions. He thought it an outstanding idea. I made the first donation to our cause, a $1,000 check made out to the *'Bishop's UN interfaith project'* so our initial seed funds could not be diverted to other needy causes.

Bishop Swing bravely pursued the vision with leadership, networking, vigor and funds raising, and built the organization that launched the **United Religions Initiative** program in 1995. URI today is a worldwide organization of 650 Interfaith Cooperation Circles in 84 countries. My Monthly URI newsletter describes activities of these groups who are working together throughout the world, not to proselytize our own faiths but to learn and respect the faith traditions of others while seeking out the universal truths and commonalities contained within the dogma and teaching doctrines and experiences of all of the great faith traditions.

Sacred Waters of the World:

In 1994, I sponsored a program to collect sacred waters from religious and spiritual places around the world in separate containers to mix together at the UN Interfaith service in 1995. We commissioned 40 special crystal vessels, engraved them, and proceeded to collect waters from sacred locations around the world as the Ganges, the Amazon River, the River Jordan, Kawaiaha'o Church springs in Hawaii, and Lourdes, France. 40 locations in all. I invited the Hawaiian spiritual delegation to stay at our home here near San Francisco for a week. I took the group to a fabric store nearby where we purchased multi-colored silk ribbons which we cut up and attached to each of the crystal vessels representing the colors of the rainbow and the peoples (red, brown, black white and yellow) of the world.

We had choirs of children from around the world enter Grace Cathedral during the ceremony in a parade, each carrying a vessel as they sang together and marched forward to pour the waters into a single symbolic gathering vessel. Representations of the mixed waters were later returned back to special locations around the world. The last three of the brightly colored vessels are here on my shelf awaiting final distribution. At my own passing, one of the three will return to Hawaii and be placed at Kawaiaha'o and off Waikiki, mingling forever with all of Karen and my family members as per the Hawaiian custom.

Interfaith Center at the San Francisco Presidio:
I also worked on the inception of the Interfaith Center at the Presidio, www.interfaith-presidio.org, a project to convert the old U.S. 6th Army's main chapel into an interfaith facility serving the needs of the faith traditions of San Francisco and the Bay Area including our First Peoples. Karen and I entertained its founders Paul and Jan Chaffee in our home for Easter dinner this year. The ICP welcomes, serves and celebrates the diverse spiritual wisdom and faith traditions of the Bay Area and is networked with interfaith groups locally and globally. The Center's core activities include developing local and global connections and **creating interfaith learning environments and resources.**

The above examples are intended to remind us of the power of ideas By boldly introducing them into the mainstream lives of important, busy, and powerful and ordinary people alike, each of us can make a difference. All goodness starts when one person takes one idea, puts it into writing, and then shares it with others. Your ideas, self-published and presented to the rest of us, could literally change the world. Through Self-Publishing, you have very powerful tools and resources at your fingertips. Use them wisely.

eBook Publishing – Special Considerations:

Once you have published a trade softcover or hardback book, there are additional considerations in reformatting your manuscript for submission for publishing as an eBook. We are focusing our initial discussion around Kindle Direct Publishing for the following reasons:

1) KPD or Kindle Direct Publishing is a wholly owned subsidiary of Amazon, separate from CreateSpace which is also a wholly owned subsidiary of Amazon.

2) CreateSpace will submit to KDP all of your information prepared and submitted for the trade softcover book including your completed manuscript, cover, and book description.

3) If you only plan to publish an eBook and not a book, you can go to KDP directly and submit your manuscript and supporting documentation. In our case, we had CreateSpace submit our completed package to KDP, and now we log onto KDP directly to complete the manuscript preparation and submit it for distribution as an eBook.

4) You have distribution options. A 90 day exclusive on Amazon comes with some benefits initially on Amazon.com, and eventually via other distributors once the initial 90 day exclusive expires.

5) http://ebook.online-convert.com/ offers tools for converting your .doc and .pdf files to .mobi and other eBook formats required for input to self-publishing sites producing eBooks for distribution.

For $79.00 Createspace will convert your basic Createspace book manuscript for suitability for publishing as an eBook through KDP. We recommend for your first eBook that you use a conversion service because it will relieve you of a lot of intense work on your part to convert your first book for eBook publishing. Your converted eBook file is provided to you for use with others eBook distribution channels.

There are many differences from standard publishing formats for physical book distribution. Specifications for Manuscript type font, pagination, Table of Contents specific page designation, and page header and footers, are not fixed for an eBook as they are for a soft or hard cover book. Formatting for an eBook requires a different group of skills over those you have learned to publish a manuscript using standard word processing software packages and techniques.

Special considerations for eBook preparation include;

eViewing PDA software has options for the eReader to select a font size and font type for preferred personal viewing.

eBooks do not use specific page numbers as with a printed book. eBooks use a relative numbering system. When an eBook font type and size are changed by the reader, the page numbers are irrelevant, so a sliding scale tied to the electronic Table of Contents adjusts itself.

The Table of Contents is electronic and links to designation headings within the document and not to specific page numbers as in a fixed page book format. The electronic TOC in the eBook links you directly to the proper section by clicking it from the TOC.

eBooks have the ability to dynamically link the eBook TOC with links selected by the reader. Incorporating this nice feature is done by KDP.

Justification is not important. eBooks will be formatted into the full left/right justification and will insert proportional spacing, so even if your input manuscript is only left justified, it will appear as fully Justified in the eBook version.

There is no best typeface font for eBook viewing. Different initial Font typefaces preferred for eBook viewing depend on the individual reader and the Author. Some stated preferences include sans-serif types as Verdana, Calibri. Times New Roman and Bookman Old Style are serif type fonts preferred by others.

KDP will prepare an eBook suitable to be viewed on a variety of platforms including: IPad, Kindle, Kindle Fire, Kindle Fire HD, Kindle Paperwhite, and an IPhone, with full color where supported on the PDA viewing device.

When viewing a book as an eBook, if you are linked to the Internet over a wireless connection live, all URL links including music, graphics and videos are activated and you can branch away to any specific web site from your eBook. And return to your reading when done.

Pricing and Royalties:

Although you can specify any price for your eBook, there are pricing limitations depending on which Royalty scheme you select. Some eBooks are limited to a top price set of $9.99 if you select the 70/30 Royalty option, 70% to you and 30% to the company.

If you want to price your eBook higher than $9.99, your royalty will be reduced to the 35/65 plan, 35% to you and 65% to the distribution companies. The 70% royalty option is only applicable for books sold to customers in the following countries: US, UK, Canada, France, Great Britain, Germany, India. Italy, Mexico, Spain, and some others. You need to check the details of your distribution pricing alternatives.

Distribution cost:

Although there are no costs to the buyer of an eBook for delivery over the Internet, the distributor will deduct a small amount from your Royalty for electronic delivery of your eBook. This generally runs around $0.10 per 1mb of data delivered. This book which is 262 pages consumes around 3mb of compressed computer storage space in the cloud, so KDP will deduct an est. $0.30 from my 70% Royalty, netting me $6.70 from the 70% of the $9.99 list price.

Updates:

Once your eBook is in distribution, it is very easy to submit updated manuscripts with changes and additions. But first you will have to go back to update your softcover book through CreateSpace and get the new version into full distribution, and then call KDP to have your book transferred over to KDP, and again it will be best to pay the one time conversion cost of $79.00 to convert your book from softcover into eBook format. Since the distribution is electronic, your new version is available online almost immediately.

Linking Kindle and Print Editions:

Many authors and publishers using KDP to publish their eBooks on Kindle also have a physical edition published through CreateSpace or another publishing house. Linking these various formats to one another in the Amazon catalog provides the ideal browsing experience for customers. During the publishing process, KDP will attempt to match title, author name, and other title information to physical counterparts available in the Amazon catalog store.

There are two ways to produce an eBook:

I. **Conversion** of an existing manuscript created for publishing a hard or softback book.

II. **Creation** of an eBook from scratch, bypassing completely the production and publishing of a hard or soft cover book

I. Conversion:

There are a number of services who will convert your manuscript into output formats required by different ePublishing companies. You can search "eBook conversion companies" for a listing of companies you can investigate. Each publisher whether it is Barnes&Noble, Google Books, Apple iBooks Author, Amazon Books, or other, they will tell you the required input format(s) for eBooks they will distribute.

http://www.ebookconversiondirectory.com/category/listings/
lists over 100 services that will assist you to convert any input manuscript format into any output format required for any of the eBook distribution companies. Conversion costs run between $0.50 to $1.00 per page from simple to complex conversions.

The Kindle Conversion Service:
KCS transforms your print-ready paperback into a Kindle eBook so your work can reach millions of Kindle and Apple readers worldwide. All elements of your paperback will be available on any Amazon Kindle reading device and on all Kindle Apps. The price varies according to the complexity including the number of imbedded links and images in your manuscript: The Basic conversion is $79.00. Complex is by quote.

The eBook produced reflects your original interior formatting and design as closely as possible to ensure that both the print and Kindle eBook versions of your work are consistent. It creates eBooks that can be viewed in color on the Aple IPads and Kindle Fire and Kindle Apps and in grayscale on all other Kindle devices. You must have a print-ready trade paperback book in the CreateSpace system first.

Your Kindle eBook will match your paperback book as closely as possible. The images will remain the same, however, in some instances, the images may be less clear and the formatting may differ slightly.

II. Creation - eBook Authoring software:

If you have no need for a hard or soft cover version of your book to be available in libraries or sold worldwide through distributors, bookstores and outlets, you can proceed directly to create your book from scratch in eBook format. Building your eBook directly eliminates the prior steps creating and publishing a softcover or hardback book.

eBook Software: (what to look for)

While there are countless aspects that determine what software is the best, there are four important categories to consider: Features, Compiling Capabilities, Ease of Use, and Help & Support. Your depth of interest in eBook publishing will determine the number of features you require.

If you are looking for a basic eBook complier application that will upload your text to the web for download or purchase, you will be able to select most any software and get the job done. However, if you are interested in customizing your creation, you should view the variety of options that are offered through the different applications available.

You can add additional features to your eBook such as music, graphics or videos. In addition to file type, the compiling capabilities of an eBook determine everything from the design of the book and its aesthetic appeal, to links and navigation.

Amazon Kindle:

http://www.amazon.com/dp/B007URVZJ6

"*Building your book for Kindle*" above is a free Kindle eBook from Amazon that describes how to use their eBook creation services.

Prices for eBook creation software to run on your desktop typically range between $29.00 and $99.00. Some allow a free download trial period to evaluate the software for your requirements.

Top ranked eBook authoring software products including reprints of their self-descriptions are listed below.

eBook Maestro   http://www.ebookmaestro.com/

Everything you need to create full-featured eBooks and other informational products can be found in eBook Maestro! EBook Maestro is a universal eBook compiler used to create any informational products (such as eBooks, Magazines, Albums, Galleries, Guides, Offline Sites, Reports, Documentations, Training Courses, Educational Materials, Tests, Quizzes, etc.). EBooks created with EBook Maestro are completely stand-alone EXE eBooks. After you compile an eBook, you get an executable file that does not require additional software or files to work with. You can include absolutely any files into your eBooks: HTML pages, Graphic Files, Java Scripts, VB Scripts, Cascade Style Sheets, Flash Files, Shockwave Files, ActiveX Files, Sound Files, Video Files, Java Applets, etc. You can create eBooks written in any languages with any character sets. The IE rendering engine is used to visualize pages. It guarantees that everything is displayed without distortions and supporting the features used in Internet Explorer.

DeskTop Author   www.desktopauthor.com

is an ebook or electronic publishing software that allows you to quickly, easily and professionally create and sell electronic publications such as eBooks, eCatalogs, ePresentations, photo albums and much more. Create multi-media powered presentations and electronic publications by embedding or streaming video, flash & VR media. You can now assign Activation Key's to your DNL DRM protected eBooks. You can sell the Activation Keys to the consumers through your own payment facility such as Pay Pal and Google Checkout. Then issue the Activation Keys to your customers together with a link to download the eBook. Copy and paste text and flow it thought multiple pages. Resize, add and re-position text boxes and text adjusts automatically: DNL eBooks created using DeskTop Author run on Windows and Apple.

eBooks Compiler   http://www.ebookscompiler.com/

Starting your ebook business is as easy as 1, 2, 3. It only takes 7 steps to create an ebook. We even give you a pre-designed ebook so all you have to do is add your own content. There is an ebook compiler user guide that covers each step with 'how to' videos if you need them covering the key areas:
    1. eBook Title   2. Select Pages   3. eBook Security   4. Design Toolbar

5. Insert Bookmarks   6. Brand Your eBook   7. Compile eBook
You get a sample ebook so all you need to do is fill it in with your content and upload.

MyeBook Maker   http://myebookmaker.com/

Create eBooks in the cloud!   Sign up and create eBooks in the cloud for free. Download your books in ePub format ready to distribute to eBook stores.   Make a New Book: Creating a new book is simple. In the members area just click New Book. You can give your book a title and author. You can also upload a cover image of you wish.   Edit Book: The eBook Content Editor allows you to write your text and add new chapters. Name your chapters and insert images, then download your book in ePub format for free.   The My Books Page allows you to update your eBook, change covers and title, preview your work in html format, and also download your eBook in ePub Format for free.

Vibosoft ePub Converter   www.vibosoft.com/epub-converter.html

Vibosoft ePub Converter, is a reliable desktop application which gives you the ability to create or make ePub eBooks from popular formats like .docx or .doc, .txt, .mobi, .prc, .pdf, and .html. After converting, you can publish the ePub files on your own websites or transfer them to your own eReaders for reading anytime and anywhere, and to your ePublisher for global distribution.
Accurately convert different file types to ePub including; Word (docx, doc), MOBI (.mobi, .prc), HTML, Text (.txt), and PDF. Preserve text contents, layouts, and images in the output file with zero loss.   Purchase for $39.95.
Never Lose Any Original Elements from Your Source Documents.
Preserve Original Elements in the Output File with No Quality Loss.
Perfectly Compatible with All Microsoft Word Versions.
Create your own ePub books in Word Doc or Docx format, an ideal format to edit files, but not the perfect file type for reading on eReaders. This ePub Converting software supports all versions of Microsoft Word.
Perfectly compatible with almost all popular eReaders on the market;
- **Apple**'s iOS devices: iPhone 5S/5C/5/4S/4/3GS, iPad 4, the new iPad, iPad mini, iPod touch,
- **Android** Phones & Tablets: Samsung, LG, HTC, Motorola.

Aspose Word: www.aspose.com
A utility to edit ePub, .net and Android file formats for eBook editing and publishing.

Altova XML Spy: www.altova.com/xmlspy.html
Altova XMLSpy® 2014 is the industry's best-selling XML editor for modeling, editing, transforming, and debugging XML-related technologies. It offers the world's leading graphical schema designer, a code generator, file converters, debuggers, profilers, full database integration, support for XSLT, XPath, XQuery, WSDL, SOAP, XBRL, JSON, and Office Open XML (OOXML) , plus Visual Studio and Eclipse integration, and more.

Costs:

Breakdown of the cost to produce: (Based on this book at 262 pages)

1	2	3	4	5	6	7
Book Type	Color	Fixed cost	Page print	Print cost	Total cost	List price
Softcover	b/w	$0.00	$0.015	$3.84	$3.84	**$18.00**
Hardcover	b/w	$8.50	$0.015	$3.84	$12.34	**$26.50**
eBook	color	$0.00	$0.000	$0.00	$0.00	**$9.99**
Softcover	color	$0.00	$0.150	$38.40	$38.40	**$52.00**
Hardcover	color	$8.50	$0.150	$38.40	$46.90	**$60.00**

1 – There are five basic book types you can specify:
    2 - Softcover   (in b/w or color)
    2 - Hardcover (in b/w or color)
    1 - eBook (in b/w or color depending on your viewer)

2 – b/w black and white (actually grayscale), or color.

3 – The fixed cost additional for hardcover books is generally $6.50 for the cover (laminate or cloth), and $2.00 for the optional dust cover.

4 – The cost to print a b/w page is $0.015 or 1.5 cents. The cost to print a color page is $0.15 or 15 cents. The cost to print a book in color in the U.S. today is prohibitively expensive. In reality you will not produce your book in color as there is no market at the $50.00-$60.00 price you will have to charge for your book to make a royalty. Only very short (20-30 page) children's books are printed in color today.

5 – The total print cost is the # of pages times the per page print cost.

6 – The total cost to produce your book is printing plus the cover. The softcover (in color) on today's POD printers is included in the estimated cost to print per page and is provided at no additional cost .

7 – The List Price is the price you set for your book to generate the acceptable royalty net to yourself after the publisher deducts its cost to produce your book and its and other distributors share.

Royalties:

Breakdown of your earned Royalties: (Based on this book at 262 pages)

Book Type	List price	Net profit	Royalty (1)	Royalty (2)	Royalty (3)	Royalty (4)
Softcover	**$18.00**	$14.16	$10.50	$7.00	$3.50	$14.00
Hardcover	**$26.50**	$14.16	$10.50	$7.00	$3.50	$14.00
eBook	**$9.99**	$9.99	na	$6.70	$6.70	

Softcover	**$52.00**	$13.60
Hardcover	**$60.00**	$13.10

(1) - The highest earned royalty is having your publisher sell the book through its own channels. In our case we get est. $10.50 for books purchased on the Createspace web site.
https://www.createspace.com/4722074

(2) - A sale through Amazon.com will net us $7.00 est. as both Createspace and Amazon take their fair share to cover their costs.

(3) - 3rd party distribution channels will take an additional royalty cut which can reduce my royalty to est. $3.50.

(4) - You can order books from the publisher at cost of close to $4.00 and sell them yourself anywhere and make up to a $14.00 profit, assuming you can get the $18.00 listing price. You can order them in bulk, store them in your garage, and then sell them on eBay, at book sales, swap meets, book showings, and on your own web site.

It is doubtful you will be selling any of your books in the color softcover or color hardcover version, even to immediate family members.

We strongly recommend that you let the professionals sell and distribute your books for you and gladly have them take their fair share of the royalties while you focus in your own area of expertise, writing books.

Traditional Publishing versus Self-Publishing:

Wise counsel from some publishing industry thought leaders…

Statistics:

Bowker _www.bowker.com_ is the world's leading provider of bibliographic information and management solutions designed to help publishers, booksellers, and libraries better serve their customers. Creators of products and services that make books easier for people to discover, evaluate, order, and experience, the company also generates research and resources for publishers, helping them understand and meet the interests of readers worldwide. Bowker, a ProQuest affiliate, is the official ISBN Agency for the United States and its territories. The company is headquartered in New Providence, New Jersey, with additional operations in England and Australia.

Bowker provides a spectrum of services for small publishers through resources such as www.selfpublishedauthor.com, www.myidentifiers.com and www.bookwire.com. To view Bowker's 2012 report on self-publishing visit www.selfpublishedauthor.com.

Marketing:

Norm Schriever: Perhaps one of the best books that will help you to Market your self-published book is _The Book Marketing Bible_.

" 'Self-publish' is no longer a bad word in the book business, thanks to the swell of authors who elect to SP to get their stories out in the world. Long gone are the days when SP was equivalent to vanity publishing, and innovations in technology and ways to share digital content are revolutionizing the industry. The bad news? Most self-published authors run full speed into a brick wall when it comes to the task of marketing and actually selling their self-published book. Let's take a look at some sobering statistics about the explosion of SP, and the all-too common collision with the real world of marketing and sales.

There were more than 391,000 self-published titles in 2012 according to Bowker. That's a 59% increase compared to the year before and a 422% increase since 2007.

It's estimated that 40% of all books are self--published these days.

The average self-published author sells less than 250 books.

Almost 20% of self-published authors report making no income at all from their books according to Digital Book World, that's 1 out of every 5 that make nothing at all.

The median income for self-published authors is reported between $1 and $4,999, which accounts for almost 65% of SP authors.

50% of all self-published authors make less than $50 on their books. 10% of SP authors account for 75% of all income in the field. Add that up: almost 85% of SP authors make under $5k per year. Only 1.8% of SP authors make over $100,000.

We can help. To be clear, these aren't magic tricks. It's about a lot of hard work and creativity smarts applied to fundamental marketing pillars. Additionally, a lot of success in book marketing has to do with shifting to the right mindset, not just what activities you undertake.

I know from 20 years of marketing experience and my journey with self-publishing and marketing two books, mistakes, victories, and all. The Book Marketing Bible is available on Amazon.com for your Kindle or eBook reader."

Traditional vs. Self-publishing is a False Dichotomy:

Nathan Bransford:
"There is no "us" vs "them." Traditional vs. self-publishing is a false dichotomy. It's an illusion created by people who either have let their frustrations get the best of them or are trying to sell you something. We're all writers trying to figure out the best way to get our books to readers. We're all on the same team.

No, the traditional publishing industry is not a hive of retrograde monsters out to steal and eat your newborn children. No, self-publishing is not a gang of unwashed crap artists trying to poison the literary well forever.

Publishing is a spectrum of choice, from traditional publishers who pay you, will handle most things for you and assume all risk in exchange for certain rights to your book, to self-publishing where you handle everything yourself, pay your own way, and adopt your own risk. And there's a whole lot more choice in between those two poles.

What's the right way? There is no right way. Some authors want to let the publishers handle things for them. Some authors want to go for print glory because that's where the bulk of readers are right now (yes, still). Some authors want the freedom of control of self-publishing. Some authors want to experiment with pricing.

And guess what: _Some authors do both_, and they always have. Even before e-publishing, many prominent authors got their start self-publishing. And many authors who used to be traditionally published moved to self-publishing. Some authors use hybrid models that combine elements of traditional and self-publishing.

There is no hundred foot wall between self-publishing and traditional publishing. Choosing one does not preclude the other, even if you feel like you're currently on the outs with traditional publishing. Or did you miss the recent seven figure book deal for the self-published nutritionist? The only way you'll be able to decide what's best for you is if you ignore the pied pipers, set aside your emotions, and think only about what's the right for your book."

Traditional Publishing versus Self-Publishing:

Courtney Milan: www.courtneymilan.com   "Choosing between self-publishing and traditional publishing methods is no easy task. Authors who want to get published have many options.

In **traditional publishing**, the author completes his or her manuscript, writes a query letter or a proposal, and submits these documents to a publishing house (or has a literary agent do this for them, if one can be acquired). An editor reads it, considers whether it is right for the house, and decides either to reject it (leaving the author free to offer it to another publisher) or to publish it. If the publishing house decides to publish the book, the house buys the rights from the writer and pays him or her an advance on future royalties. The house puts up the money to design and package the book, prints as many copies of the book as it thinks will sell, markets the book, and finally distributes the finished book to the public.

The process is a bit different for **self-publishing**. An author who decides to self-publish basically becomes the publisher. The author must proofread the final text and provide the funds required to publish the book as well as the camera-ready artwork. The author is responsible for marketing and distributing the book, filling orders, and running advertising campaigns. In the past, the author had to decide on the number of copies to print, sometimes resulting in stacks of unsold books gathering dust in the garage! Fortunately, the Print on Demand (POD) technology now used by some self-publishing companies means that authors can have fewer copies printed—only as many as they need, in fact.

Having looked at traditional publishing versus self-publishing, ask yourself some tough questions about what is best for you, your intentions, and your manuscript. Are you willing to play the waiting game in order to earn a large advance from a traditional publisher? Or are control of your manuscript and a quick turnaround more important?

The good news is that the available tools—POD, the Internet, and online booksellers—are leveling the playing field between traditionally published and self-published books. **Authors now have more options**."

Eight Trends that favor the Self-Publishing industry:

We end with eight Predictions for the future:

1. The Information economy is vibrant, healthy and growing.
2. The all electronic banking revolution will soon be here to speed up global commerce.
3. The accelerating rate of growth of information requires new indexing and linking techniques to convert information into useful knowledge.
4. Our personal experiences, through self-publishing, contribute to converting information into knowledge that the world needs to succeed.
5. Indexing engines (tools) and determined people are increasingly required to convert information into useful knowledge.
6. Future economic cycles and generational crises must be expected. We will deal with them when they occur.
7. Spiritual linkages uniting the souls of the people of this world will help to keep us centered and sane as the knowledge base explodes almost beyond our comprehension. Organizations like the United Religions Initiative and the Interfaith Center at the Presidio will use these same technologies to spread their messages and achieve their vision of a world united by the common spiritual base at the core of what it is to be human.
8. The economics of micro self-publishing are in our favor as it becomes one of the true growth industries in our society that increases employment and generates new wealth that we can share.

Now is an excellent time to get started self-publishing that first book you have always imagined. You need the world, and the world needs you. Enjoy! Celebrate! It is a big, fun, glorious, exciting, risky and at times downright scary world out here. Our growing legions of first time self-publishers, hopefully soon to include yourself, are destined to help us understand and manage these global changes at the same time as we contribute to them.

About the Author
Jon H. Larson

Jon, Zachary, Derek, Annie, Hien and Karen

Jon's two "most important achievements":
- Taking good care of my life partner Karen for 50 years
- Being Grandpa to Zach and Annie

Born in 1941 in Honolulu, Hawaii
Raised: Honolulu, Hawaii   Graduated Punahou School in 1959

Education: *Yale University* – BS IA/EE Indust. Admin., Elect. Engin.

Military Service: *199th Fighter Interceptor Squadron*
                   HANG - Hawaii Air National Guard

Personal:
Married for 50 years to Karen Brown of Rochester, New York
Son Derek Larson age 48

Residence: Tiburon, California since 1975.

I have come to view life not as a straight line forward from childhood, gaining strength and proficiency and accumulating power and earning capacity, peaking at mid-age and then a slow decline back to impotence and nothingness.

Life is more like a chambered nautilus in which we return (circle around) over and over again through past experiences, always gaining expanded consciousness, understanding and meaning, and retaining the key lessons/learning's of life that remain deeply buried within us.

These lessons become the essence of our souls and make each of us worthy and unique on the planet. We remain vital and involved, less powerful physically but more powerful mentally, and important until the day we leave this sweet Earth.

Then we continue on through....
- The trees we have planted,
- The people we have educated and assisted with simple kindnesses along the way,
- The children we helped bring into this world and nurtured while providing them with roots and wings of their own, and
- **The books we have written.**

I have eight more mostly completed books stored in my desktop computer at home, needing only final assembly with a word processor to ready them for self-publishing. Using the tools and techniques described in this book, I can get all eight of them self-published easily by my Yale 55th reunion in 2018. That is only two books a year.

Life offers each of us many gifts. I have come to believe that perhaps the greatest gift that comes to a man in his life, besides the gift of life itself from his mother and father, is the love of a good woman. It can come free and easy, with unexpected suddenness, but it always takes years of work to deserve and keep. Barbara Bush is right when she says *"Any successful marriage over time is an 80/20 proposition, and each of you gives the 80%."* Putting our life force energy into writing books, over time, yields the same benefits for ourselves and others.

We have all been given a wonderful gift, the ability **to self-publish our wisdom for the benefit of others and those who come after us.**

Jon H. Larson - (Personal essay)   (shameless self-promotion)

I was born and raised in the Hawaiian Islands. I was most fortunate to experience three of the world's great educational institutions; Punahou School in Hawaii, Yale University, and the IBM Corporation.

For over 40 years, I held a number of positions in computer and network design engineering, marketing, project management and consulting around the U.S. and abroad, through IBM and on my own as a consultant. Mid career I was the co-founder and president/CEO of MEDICOM Corporation.

My most prized public recognition was winning the yearly President's Award as the #1 recognized contributor to Total Quality Management in U.S. industry by the Association for Quality and Participation, dedicated to improving workplaces through quality and participation practices.

<u>Self:</u>   I enjoy regular swims at the local community pool to stay healthy. I am writing six books and look forward to electronic publishing them over the coming years. I derive immense enjoyment from re- reading old classics in my library and the thriving hummingbird farm in my back yard.

<u>Creating wealth</u>:   I am managing partner of a small VC company IRPLLC which invests my own and partners capital in a managed portfolio of 29 startup and early stage companies over a broad range of products and services. The work keeps me young, in touch, involved and relevant.

<u>Non-profit mentorship</u>:   I manage our Larson Family Foundation, a non-profit 501(c)(3) that nurtures 25 community social programs and non-profit organizations whose missions include interfaith education, cultural preservation, spiritual enlightenment, and environmental conservation.

<u>Life's special blessings</u>:   Karen and I continue to enjoy our beautiful old family home of 40 years overlooking the Bay in Tiburon just north of San Francisco. We enjoy easy access year round to a full schedule of subscriber memberships in the ballet, opera, symphony, performing theater arts, speaker   series, museums, and live performances.

<u>Family:</u>   My two sisters Helen and Gail have both enriched my life immeasurably. No father is prouder of his son than I of Derek and his wife Hien. And being a grandparent (for me to Zachary and Annie) is God's reward for our difficult and often imperfect life's work here on earth.

<u>Life's greatest gift</u>:   The greatest gift that comes to a man in his life, besides the gift of life itself from his Mother and Father, is the love of a good woman. I have been most fortunate and blessed to have shared my last 50 years with Karen, as deep, complex, intelligent, funny, mysterious, and loving a woman as God ever placed on our green Earth."

<u>Life's second greatest gift:</u>   **Grandchildren**

Jon H. Larson - (CV)   (more shameless self-promotion)

Jon has served many roles including founder, chairman, president or director of 501(c)(3) non-profits including *Charity Enablers Foundation, Iliahi Foundation of Hawaii, TAO Education Foundation, Bay Area Association for Quality* and *Participation, PE Homeowners Association, United Religions Initiative - URI, Californians for Missing Children*, and the *Larson Family Foundation*.

Jon is a managing partner of *Investment Recovery Partners LLC*. He places investment capital for himself and 28 Partners in 29 seed and early stage companies where he maintains ongoing advisor/mentor relationships through liquidity of each investment. These diverse companies include; *ActiveLight.TV* - computer/internet integrated digital flat panel display technology and narrow band advertising, *FusionIO* - NAND flash-based ioMemory technologies for powering high performance computing systems and data centers, *ArmedZilla* – social networking for the U.S. military, *Hoku Scientific* - hydrogen fuel cell and poly-silicon solar power research and manufacturing, *Language Weaver* - statistical machine translation of foreign language pairs, *Forensic Logic* - cross jurisdictional crime analysis and tracking, *NanoPoint* – micro-biology bio-photonics and intra-cell imaging, *BioVentrix* - medical instrumentation for minimally invasive surgical repair of CHF heart disease, *Global Bionic Optics* - massive depth of field lens technology for security and biometrics and medical diagnostics, *Renewable Energy Resources*, *Osage Exploration* and 15 domestic oil and gas projects.

Additional early stage investments include; *Eureka Genomics* - advanced low cost genomic DNA sequence analysis, *JP Renew* - nutraceutical health products based on plant sources from the ocean, *SynerTech* - software-based authentication technology for wireless devices, *SpaceData* - marine seismic ship-to-shore data transfer using the TDRSS satellite channels, *American Beef Processing* - automated fat separation for low-fat pathogen-free ground beef production, *Phloronol* –ocean based pharmaceutical treatments for neurological diseases including PD and Alzheimer's, and *PepTide Biosciences* - non-toxic cost-effective proprietary treatment protocols for autoimmune and immune-mediated diseases and the discovery of new peptides via combinatorial libraries, and *Neurotrope* - a diagnostic test for early stage Alzheimer's disease.

At **IBM Corporation**, Jon held a number of positions in computer engineering, marketing, project management and consulting around the U.S. and abroad. IBM customers served include; *Southern Pacific, American President Lines, Pacific Motor Trucking, Blue Cross of California, British National, Ferrocarriles Nacionales de Mexico, Union Pacific, Canadian National, ConRail,* and *Sprint*.

Jon was co-founder and president/CEO of *MEDICOM Corporation* which he built from base zero into the largest private online medical data processing network in northern California. Jon served as co-managing Partner of *Illinois Energy Partners LLC, Pioneer Energy Partners, Inc.* and *Five Nines Capital Management LLP.* He held consulting positions in computer systems and network architecture design and technical projects management at *Sterling Executive Search, Tecxel Hospital Services Corp., Levi Strauss, MCI/SystemHouse, AAA of California (CSAA),* and *Electronic Data Systems - (EDS).*

WWW.YALE63.ORG
"THE SEASONS OF OUR LIVES"

To Yale '63 with love,
Jon Larsen

About the Author   257

Family room

Master bedroom

Karen's sewing room

Jon's office

Coat closet

Back seat of Jon's 2002 Saab

Jon and Karen's home of 40 years,,, books, books and more books.

The corner of Jon's office at home

- ➤ Three engraved crystal vessels of *Sacred Waters of the World* from the 1995 United Nations Interfaith service at Grace Cathedral in San Francisco, with silk ribbons symbolizing the colors of the rainbow and all of God's children.
- ➤ An old Navajo blanket from Santa Fe, NM.
- ➤ A wood box hand carved in Sweden in 1892 by my great grandfather Carl Starkenberg Larson (top).
- ➤ An 1850's Hawaiian iliahi sandalwood box hand carved in China and passed on to me in 1948 by my proper English maiden great aunties Anne and Eva Hadley, originally from Newtown Square, PA. Eva worked for a British trading company in Japan and Anne taught English to the children of Hawaiian royalty at <u>Lahainaluna School</u> on Maui in the later 1800's before the overthrow of the monarchy in 1893.
- ➤ A photo of the Dalai Lama taken by my son Derek in 1991 at a global Buddhist Kalachakra in the Indus River Valley in India.
- ➤ A mother and a baby Dolphin made from blue crystal glass.
- ➤ Two Hawaiian leis made of Kukui nuts, and one orange bird feather Hawaiian Royalty lei (simulated in silk), handmade by my Punahou classmates for our 40th reunion in 1999.
- ➤ Bookshelf containing over 500 books purchased over the years.

Technology Trends and Publishing:

The features and prices quoted throughout this book are all subject to change. By this reading they could already be significantly different than shown herein. Future versions of this book will reflect the then current features and pricing. Before use, they must be checked with the vendors themselves for current pricing, features and availability.

The book publishing industry continues to change and adapt. Book publishing and distribution techniques are rapidly changing. Self-publishing is a fast paced component of the publishing industry that continues to absorb and exploit the latest in computer and data communications technologies driven over the expanding Internet.

Companies that cannot adapt to technology developments in this industry will have a difficult time surviving.

On the other hand, there are tremendous growth and profitability avenues for the companies that are able to make changes and adapt and take advantage of the newest technological developments to assist Authors to publish their work.

Overall the industry has never been more vibrant. There are millions of potential unpublished Authors out there who need the latest tools and services of Publishers and Distributors as the knowledge base of the human condition grows exponentially.

Hop onboard. It promises to be quite a ride for all of us.
All the best,

Jon H. Larson
Tiburon, California

THE JON AND KAREN LARSON FAMILY FOUNDATION

CHARITY ENABLERS FOUNDATION

Interfaith education
Cultural preservation
Spiritual enlightenment
Environmental conservation, protection and restoration

The Jon and Karen Larson Family Foundation (LFF) / Charity Enablers Foundation (CEF), is a private family foundation operated for public benefit charitable purposes only. LFF/CEF provides both financial and non-financial support including organizational development, and administrative and entrepreneurial assistance to non-profit organizations and individuals whose community activities fall within the above four general areas.

a California charitable nonprofit (501c3) public benefit corporation

PO Box 751, Tiburon, CA 94920
Calif. Corporation id#: 02237360   Federal EIN#: 68-0460563
Web site: **www.lff1.org**

Made in the USA
Charleston, SC
31 May 2014